Prairie Rose and Rosebud

by Lela DeMille

Light and Life Press
999 College Avenue
Winona Lake, Indiana 46590

Printed in the United States of America
by Light and Life Press
Winona Lake, Indiana 46590

Copyright 1988
Light and Life Press
ISBN 0-89367-140-1

Contents

Preface

This is the second book in a series which tells the story of my mother. In the main it is a factual account. I have tried to fill in with things of historical interest. For example, I do not *know* that my mother made lye soap, but since it was the accepted practice in that era, I assume she did.

I trust you will enjoy sharing Elba and Alma's life for a time and that you may be blessed by their love one for the other and for God.

Dedicated, with love, to my dear sister, Neva.

Acknowledgements to:

Memories Are Forever — Manor and District Historical Society.

World Book Encyclopedia

Joy of Cooking, Rombauer, Becker, Bobbs-Merrill

Myrtle Taylor, daughter of Henry and Harriet Cudmore, who supplied much information about her family, home, and the area around Cannington Manor.

Many thanks to Marian Groesbeck and Wilmer Bartel for their helpful encouragement, and to my kind typist, Lori Caswell.

Chapter 1

Time of the Singing of Birds

The winter of 1905 gradually wore away. The crows returned with their promise of spring. One day Elba came in the cabin with his hands held behind his back. "Close your eyes, Alma. I've got something for you."

Neva came running. "Is it a 'sprise, Papa?" She tried to look behind Papa's back, but he twisted aside. "It's a 'sprise for Mama," he replied, holding out a branch of pussy willows.

"Oh, aren't they darling! I love pussy willows. Where did you find them?" Alma asked excitedly.

"Out by the slough," Elba said, happy

in her pleasure. "I thought you would like them."

"Let me see! Let me see! Are they real little kitties?"

Elba laughed. "Not really, Kitten, they're furry like kittens. Guess that's why they're called pussy willows."

Alma put them in a vase. "*Now* I believe that spring is on the way."

Several days later, Alma stood at the window watching Neva, in her wellington boots, splashing through the puddles. "She'll be all muddy when she comes in," Alma said aloud. "Poor dear, she's been cooped up so long she doesn't know what to do with herself." She laughed at Neva's antics with her dog, Girl.

"If I didn't have to finish this laundry, I'd be out there myself!"

She turned back to her tub with a sigh. She placed Elba's work shirt on the washboard, rubbed it with lye soap and scrubbed it up and down.

The door opened and Elba came in, his face all smiles. He bowed to her and pointed to the open doorway. "Your carriage awaits, my queen. We're going for a ride."

"Elba! I'm washing!"

"Well, I guarantee the clothes will be right here when we get back."

"That's what I'm worried about," she said.

He took her in his arms. "Come on, Dear, it's such a nice day, and you need a change. Tell you what, I'll help you with the washing when we get back." He untied her apron strings and turned her around with a pat on her seat.

"Tidy your hair, get your hat, and we'll be off. I'll call Neva." He went outside and found Neva making mud pies in a puddle.

"Want to go for a ride?"

"Oh, yes," she said jumping up. "We going in the wagon?"

"Nope!"

She looked up at him. His eyes were twinkling and he was smiling.

"Ride the horses?" she asked, her eyebrows lifting in inquiry.

"Nope!"

Her forehead was a puzzled frown. "How're we going?"

"You'll see!" he said and touched the end of her nose. "Here, let's wash your hands and face at the pump." He led her over to the iron pump. "Stand back a little so you don't get all splashed, and hold out your hands." He pumped the handle up and down, and a stream of water poured over Neva's hands.

"It's cold!" She hunched her shoulders and shivered. Elba came around the pump and washed her hands and face.

"Here, I'll wipe your face on my handkerchief. You don't need a towel for your hands. Just shake them like this." He shook the water from his hands and rubbed them together.

"Now let's see if Mama's ready."

Meanwhile, Alma had dried her hands and tidied her hair. *It will be nice to get out,* she thought, *but I hate the thought of that bumpy old wagon and that high spring seat.* She ran her hands over her distended stomach and said, "I don't know how *you* will enjoy the rough ride."

As if in response, the little one within gave a mighty kick. "Ouch!" she said and picked up her hat. "You don't have to be so emphatic about it."

As she left the house, Alma pinned her hat to her luxuriant brown hair with a long, pearl-handled hatpin. Her cheeks were flushed from hurrying and the prospect of the ride.

She stopped in her tracks. Her hand flew to her mouth. Her eyes grew big as they took in a beautiful driving horse and new buggy.

"Elba! Where did you get the horse and buggy?"

"I bought it," he said pleased with her reactions. "Didn't I say your carriage was waiting?"

"It's ours! It's ours!" Neva was clapping her hands and jumping up and down. "I wanted to tell you, but Papa wouldn't let me."

"I wanted to surprise you," he said with his lopsided grin.

"Well! You certainly did that." She flashed him a radiant smile.

"Meet Nettie," Elba said pointing to the horse.

Nettie was a small bay mare with slender legs and dainty Arabian head. Alma stroked the horse's proudly arched neck. "You're just beautiful, Nettie, just beautiful." She turned to Elba. "Elba, you're crazy, but I love it. I guess I'm too serious and duty-bound. You're good for me."

"I should hope so, young lady." He took her arm and helped her into the buggy. Neva hopped in beside her and Elba stepped up and took the reins from the dashboard.

"You're full of surprises, aren't you, Elba Swayze, and I do feel like a queen." She gave a happy sigh and threw her head back to let the sun shine full on her face. Then she giggled. "No, I feel more like a schoolgirl playing hooky, and it's a delicious feeling."

"You look like one too." Elba brushed her cheek with his lips and slapped the reins on Nettie's flank. "Your cheeks are like roses. My prairie rose!" Alma snuggled close.

Neva was ecstatic. She talked or sang all the way. That the adults were engaged in their own conversation and paid little attention to what she said didn't seem to bother her.

The warm chinook breeze fanned Alma's brow and loosened wisps of hair at her temples. They fell in attractive half-curls upon her cheeks. "This is lovely!" she whispered.

Elba pointed to some birds in the field. "The redwing blackbirds are back."

"What's that verse about the time of the singing of birds is come?" Alma queried.

"H-m-m," Elba mused. "I think it's from the Song of Solomon. It goes something like this — 'For, lo, the winter is past. . . . The flowers appear on the earth; The time of the singing of birds is come,' "

"Yes," Alma said dreamily, "the time of the singing of birds." She was thinking of the robins and wrens and thrushes back home. "Spring is such an alive season isn't it? In Ontario, the tulips and jonquils and crocuses will be a riot of color." She sat very quietly for a time.

Glancing sidewise at her, Elba saw a tear trickle down her cheek. He put an arm around her. "You homesick? You seemed miles away."

She smiled at him. "I was thinking about the apple orchard. How I would love to smell an apple blossom again. 'The flowers appear on the earth,'" she repeated, "but I guess we won't see many flowers here."

"Oh-h-h?" Elba looked at her knowingly. "Just wait till we pass this slough."

"Why? What is it?" she cried, excited as a child.

"Just wait and see!" He tapped the tip of her nose. As they passed the end of the slough, Neva's quick eyes picked up a shiny blanket of grey over the whole prairie. "What is it, Papa? What're all those grey things shining in the sun?"

"Why don't you go and see?" Elba reined Nettie in, and Neva was out before the buggy had really stopped. She ran to the little grey things and fell on her knees. "Mama, come. Look, little flowers in fur coats."

"Flowers?" Alma said incredulously. Elba jumped out of the buggy and lifted her down. There they were, dainty mauve flowers with bright yellow centers and, as Neva said, in grey fur coats.

"Wild crocuses, how beautiful!" Alma picked one and smelled it, smoothing a finger over the soft outer coat. "And how appropriate to the prairie." She smiled at Elba as they watched Neva, wild with delight, rush from one patch of blossoms to the next, picking in reckless abandon. It didn't matter if only the head came off, she was picking flowers for Mama!

"She's just wasting them, Elba. Shouldn't we stop her?"

"She's having fun, and there are millions of them. I don't think Mother Nature minds a bit."

Finally Neva came back to them, her apron bulging with crocuses, her face radiant with the joy of living. "For you, Mama." She dumped the flowers on the ground beside Alma.

"Thank you, dear. I guess I won't lack for flowers for a while." She carefully selected with longer stems, enough for several bouquets, and left the heads and headless on the ground.

"I feel like a new person, Elba," she said as they drove home in the buggy.

16

"I'm glad you persuaded me to come."

"I'm glad you came, too. Now, I suppose, I'll have to keep my promise and help you finish that washing."

"Well, I should say so."

As they hung the clothes outside, Alma commented, with a clothespin in her mouth, "This is different from hanging them out in the winter time. I used to nearly cry with the pain of my cold fingers, and then when I brought the clothes in, they were still stiff as boards with the frost."

"I know, Alma, it's a rugged country and only the hardy survive."

"Well, you seem to be surviving. I think you're putting on weight."

"Wouldn't be surprised at all." Elba took his cap off and ran a hand through his hair. Alma loved the way it fell in a deep wave over his forehead.

"With your good cooking and all the blessings I have, I'm a happy man. If only you enjoyed the prairie more."

"Don't worry about me. I'm fast beginning to love its vastness and freedom. It does have a beauty all its own that is captivating. Give me a year or two and I'll be a genuine prairie lover.

They walked back to the cabin swinging the clothespin bag between them.

"Come Sunday, we're going back to church over near Cannington-Manor," Elba announced that night at supper. "And we'll go every Sunday we can until the snow comes again."

Alma's face lit up. "I've missed the Christian fellowship during the winter more than anything else. It will be wonderful to be in church again. I enjoy our family prayer time, but there is something about a group of believers worshiping together that just lifts me."

"Where're we goin'?" Neva wriggled herself in between Elba's knees and pulled on his suspenders to get his attention.

"We're going to church and Sunday school again, and there'll be lots of other kids there."

"Goody! Then I'll see my friend, Jennie Fox who gave me my puppy, won't I Mama?"

Chapter 2

Renewal

Sunday was a gorgeous day. The long drive in the warm sunshine was relaxing and enjoyable. Alma felt the sun warming her back and shoulders. Saucy gophers stood tall and eyed them curiously, scurrying into their holes when the buggy approached. Jack rabbits, their white winter coats discarded for grey spring ones, hopped away over the prairie wool. Meadowlarks filled the spring air with their liquid notes.

In the distance they saw the familiar white church with its steeple pointing skyward. Buggies, wagons and democrats were converging on it from various trails.

Elba let Alma and Neva out at the door and drove on to put Nettie in the horse barn.

Mary Fox was standing just outside the door, where she welcomed Alma and Neva with a friendly smile and handshake. "Alma, I'm so glad you could come. We've been wondering how you survived the cold winter." She turned to Neva, "Hello, Neva. Would you like to go with Jennie to her class?"

Neva held back, suddenly shy among so many people, but Jennie came running up and took her hand. "Come on to my class. You'll be my fish. You'll like it. How's Girl?"

Neva didn't know whether she wanted to be a fish or not, but if Jennie said so it must be all right. They went off happily together.

When Elba came, Mary and her husband Jack greeted him, and they all chose a seat in the church together.

Alma looked around at the unadorned walls, plain wooden floor, rough plank pews, and the simple pine pulpit at the front. As usual, her mind went back to the church her father had pastored in Tillsonburg with the beautiful red carpet streamers in the aisles, and the highly polished oak pulpit so lovingly formed by her father's hands. But the spirit was the same here as it had been back home.

Soon she was lost in the simple worship service.

In the absence of the regular preacher, who came only once a month, the service was led by Mr. Cudmore, Sr. He read a familiar portion of scripture in John 11. "I am the resurrection and the life; he that believeth in me, though he were dead, yet shall he live: And whosoever liveth and believeth in me shall never die. Believest thou this?"

He then spoke of the miracle of spring which to the farmers especially brings new hope and courage. After the grey-white barrenness of winter comes the renewal of life. The life-giving sap flows up the trunk of the trees into all the branches to burst their buds into delicate shades of green. The brown grass turns green, flowers appear over the prairies, and the songbirds return to delight music-starved ears.

"As we draw close to Jesus," the speaker continued, "He draws near to us with renewal of life and energy. The warmth of His love spreads through us and causes growth in grace and understanding and faith."

It was a simple message given by a simple, direct man, but Alma felt refreshed.

After the service, the kindly folk gathered around Elba and Alma to renew their friendships. Alma recognized some of the young people who had come carolling at Christmas.

"Come and see us sometime," Mary said in parting. "We're not all that far away." Neva and Jennie waved and called to each other as far as they could be heard.

"I knew I missed church," Alma said as they drove home, "but I didn't realize how dry a person can get without the reviving and refreshing of spirit that comes from worshipping together with others."

"I agree! The apostle Paul knew what he was saying when he exhorted us 'not to forget the assembling of ourselves together'."

Alma rested her head on Elba's shoulder. "I like those people. There's a strength about them. They're friendly and open and make me feel a part of them. I'm glad to belong." She breathed a sigh of deep contentment.

"The prairies bring out the best in people. You know what I mean? A spirit of oneness as though we're all in this together. Folks are friendly and helpful

— do anything to help a neighbor," Elba commented.

Neva came out of her daydreams long enough to ask, "How many sleeps till Sunday, Mama?"

"Oh, not that again!" Alma said under her breath. "I'll hear that song every day from now till next Sunday."

"Well, at least she likes Sunday school," Elba said in his matter of fact way. "That's one more thing to be thankful for."

24

Chapter 3

Stovepipe Cleaning

Alma was singing as she went about her work in the little cabin one sunshiny day in May.

"It's housecleaning time," she said to Neva who was playing with her dolly on the doorstep.

"I want to clean too." Neva put her doll away and stood ready to help.

"All right, you can help if you want to." Alma thought a moment. "I know, your job can be to clean the outhouse."

Neva's face lit up. "All by myself?" she asked eagerly.

Alma smiled. "Yes, all by yourself. Then you can show Papa what a good job you did."

"What do I do?" Neva stood on one leg

then the other, eager to begin.

"Take the broom and sweep down all the cobwebs from the ceiling and in the corners. You'll have to stand on the seat to reach the ceiling so be sure the covers are firmly on the holes so you don't fall in."

"I will, Mama. I'll be careful."

"Then sweep the seat and the floor."

Carrying the broom, Neva hurried proudly to the outdoor toilet, a large two-seater.

Alma smiled as she watched her go. *She loves to help,* Alma thought, *and she's proud to be given a project all her own.*

The curtains came down next. Alma washed them and hung them on the line to dry in the bright sunlight. With soap and warm water, she washed the windows and shined them with an old towel.

When Neva came back with the broom, Alma gave her a small bucket of soapy water, a cloth, and scrub brush, to use in scrubbing the outhouse seat and floor.

Then Alma took the broom to attack the dust and cobwebs in the cabin which had accumulated on the ceiling and in the corners during the long winter months. She was standing on the table reaching the highest part of the ceiling when Elba came in for a drink.

"Now I *know* spring is here. What is it about spring that creates in you women this insatiable urge to clean house?"

Alma glanced down at him and wrinkled her nose. "Just the same urge that makes you men itch to get on the land, I guess."

"I made a trip to the outhouse and was informed by another industrious female that I couldn't come in because I would track up her clean floor." He shook his head and continued. "I ask you, what is a mere male to do?"

"Poor dear!" she mocked, "you are having a bad time."

Her cheeks were flushed from the exertion. A wisp of dark hair escaped from the kerchief she had tied on her head, and there was dust on her nose.

"You look adorable," he said, love shining in his grey eyes.

"Oh, Elba! In this get-up? I look awful." She gave a swipe at him with her broom.

"You be careful, young lady. You could lose your balance standing up there." She stuck out her tongue at him and continued sweeping cobwebs.

Elba removed the teapot from the top of the warming oven and poured himself a cup of leftover tea. He shoved his cap back on his head and leaned against the kitchen cabinet standing with his feet crossed.

"Do you know," he said reluctantly, "we should clean the stovepipe before you get everything spick and span in here."

Alma dropped the broom. "I forgot about that terrible job. It's so messy. There'll be soot everywhere."

"We'll be as careful as we can," he promised and helped her down from the table.

When Neva finished her scrubbing job, she dragged Papa off to admire her work.

"Well, I declare," he said rubbing his chin, "if this isn't as shiny as a new pin. I didn't know you were such a good helper." He tousled her hair.

She looked up at him, her face radiant from his praise. "But it still stinks," she said disgustedly and held her nose.

"I've got a cure for that. There's an old bucket by the rain barrell. We'll get that and the fire shovel and go down to the barn to get some lime. Then we will pour a shovelful of lime down each hole. That helps the smell.

28

"Oh, good. That'll be better."

"We have to be careful now, not to spill lime all over the clean seat and floor."

Back in the house, Elba put his hand on the stovepipe to test it. "I think it's cool enough to handle." He pulled a chair up beside the stove. Standing on the chair, he banged his hand against the pipe several times to loosen the soot and let it fall down.

"Get the dustpan and hold it under the pipe, Alma please. I'll disconnect the pipe and lift it down."

Elba carefully tried to disconnect a length of upper pipe from the bottom portions and remove it from the chimney. It was stuck. He tried to turn and twist it and at the same time give a little tug. It wouldn't budge. He twisted more and gave a harder tug and all of a sudden it did move, more than he expected. Out came the stovepipe and down came the soot! Over both of them, over the chair, over the stove, and all over the floor!

At first Alma could think of nothing more than the work of cleaning it up.

"Oh, Elba, what a mess!"

"Oh, brother!" he said. "I didn't expect it was going to give way so suddenly. Sorry!"

Alma looked up at him and burst out laughing. Elba's face was black. Soot clung to his eyelashes and moustache. The whites of his eyes and his teeth glistened in contrast to his face. He was spitting the soot from his mouth.

"I'm glad *you* think it's funny," he said peevishly. Puffs of soot streamed out as he spoke each word.

Alma laughed till the tears came to her eyes. She wiped them on her white coverall apron, which came away streaked with black.

"Am I all soot, too?" She put her hand to her face.

"I've seen you look cleaner." Elba laughed. "You didn't think you were going to get off scot-free, did you?"

Elba carried the length of pipe out to the ashpile where he banged it and cleaned it out with a long stick.

Alma came out with an old rag, and they tried to flick the soot off each other. "The rest will have to come off with soap and water," Alma said, still giggling. "Oh, you do look funny!"

"That soot sure made a mess on the floor, Alma. Sorry."

"I was planning to scrub it anyway. I'll just have to scrub a little harder around the stove."

"Alma, what I came in to tell you when I found you housecleaning was that it's time for the unveiling of the rosebush we planted last year. Do you want to be there to watch, or do you just want me to bring you a report?"

"Oh, I want to be there. I want to see for myself. Please wait until I finish scrubbing."

"All right," Elba said, "call me when you're ready. I'm going to the well to wash some of this stuff off."

Alma poured warm water into the scrub bucket. Then she scrubbed the plain pine floorboards with strong lye soap until they were clean and glistening.

When Alma called Elba to unwrap the rosebush, her face reflected her worry. "Do you think it has survived the winter?" she asked him.

He rubbed his chin with the back of his hand. "I think it has, but can't promise."

Alma glanced at him askance. "How anything can live through that long cold winter I'll never understand."

"Well, we lived through it, didn't we? And the cow and horses, they survived."

"Oh, I know, silly, but we were

31

indoors. I mean shrubs and grass and things."

"I *know* what you mean." He took her face in his hands. "I was only teasing. Even if it doesn't survive, I still have *my* rose. A dusty rose today, I must admit, but still my rose."

She slipped her arms around his neck. "I love you, Elba."

He drew her close and kissed her pretty lips, "I love you, too, dear. You're my very life!"

She rested her head on his broad chest and heard the rhythmic beating of his heart. "We aren't rich in earthly things, but we are rich in love and happiness."

"We are that," he agreed. "With God's great love and our love for each other and Neva, we are surely blessed."

Alma patted her protruding abdomen and said, "And don't forget this little one. It sure doesn't let *me* forget. The way it kicks you'd think it was practicing for a football match." She laughed.

Elba slid his hands down and gently caressed her tummy. "No. I mustn't forget you, whoever-you-are in there. We're going to give you lots of loving too."

Alma sighed happily and said, "Let's

go and see how the rosebush fared."

Elba called to Neva who was playing with Girl. "Do you want to come and see us uncover the rosebush?"

She came running, Girl jumping at her heels. "Are we going to wake up the rose?"

Elba cut the bark rope that held the covering in place. Then he carefully unrolled the hay. The plant was dry and dead. The leaves which had been so healthy last fall were brown and came away with the hay. Alma's heart sank. She had been hoping so much that it would have survived. She stood looking down at the dry plant, fighting to keep back the tears. Elba didn't say anything.

Neva knelt down beside the plant and said, "Lookit, Mama, a baby one!"

Elba and Alma dropped down beside her. Sure enough, a tiny green shoot was forcing its way through the dead-looking root.

"It's alive!" Alma cried joyously. "Oh, Elba, it's going to live!"

"For your sake, I'm very glad." He put an arm around her to help her up. "Someday you'll be picking roses from it, I hope."

"I hope so. I can hardly wait to smell a rose again."

Elba smiled down at her and said mysteriously, "You won't have to wait for these to bloom before you can smell a rose."

"What *do* you mean, Elba?"

"Just wait till next month and I'll show you."

Alma coaxed and cajoled but Elba would say no more.

Chapter 4

Prairie Roses

The month of June came with its long days and short nights. It was difficult for Alma to believe that at ten o'clock at night it was still light. In fact, it seemed to her that from sundown until sunup (about four a.m.) it was never truly dark. The coal oil lamps that had burned so many hours during the long winter days were scarcely lit. She was hardly into bed and asleep before it was time to get up again.

The many hours of sunlight each day made the crops and gardens fairly jump ahead. Alma spent a great deal of time hoeing the vegetables.

The busy rush of spring activities had eased a little, and Elba was now breaking more virgin prairie to be ready for planting next spring.

When Alma went to the doorway to call Elba and Neva for supper, she saw them coming up from the barn carrying the milk pail between them and Girl running alongside. Alma's heart always lifted at the sight of them.

After supper Elba said, "Leave the dishes a while, Alma, and come for a little walk with me."

Alma hesitated a moment so Elba said, "Or would you rather go for a ride?"

"Oh, no, you're tired, and Nettie is away out in the pasture. I'll walk. It will do me good, but I don't promise to go very far."

"No, we won't go far. There's something I want you to see over by the pasture." He took her arm as they walked along together, Neva and Girl leading the way.

"She sure loves that dog," Elba said. "You never see the one without the other when Neva is outside."

"Yes. It was a lovely thing Jennie did for Neva. Every child needs a pet. Wish we had something we could give Jennie sometime." She thought a moment then said, "I suppose I could knit her a scarf and toque for Christmas. She might like that."

"I'm sure she would," Elba agreed.

As they came near the pasture Alma sniffed. "What's that fragrance I smell?"

"What does it smell like?" She wasn't looking at Elba and missed his knowing glance.

"I'm not sure. There must be some flowering bush or some blossoms around here."

"Here they are, Mama," Neva called, trying to pick a flower. "Ouch! They got prickers!"

Elba took out his jack-knife and cut a branch. "A prairie rose for my rose." He handed it to Alma.

"A rose?" she said incredulously. "A *wild* rose?"

"Yep," Elba grinned. "Remember I promised you would smell a rose before your bush blossomed?"

"You were thinking of these!" Her face was a study of surprise and pleasure.

She gazed at the dainty rose-coloured petals, bordering the round sunshine-yellow center. She lifted it to her nose and sniffed. Then she breathed in a long steady breath as though she could not get enough of the elusive sweetness of its fragrance. With her finger she traced the serrated edges of the small green leaves.

At last she raised a radiant face to Elba, tears shining in her brown eyes. "Beautiful!" she exclaimed. "Absolutely beautiful."

Elba's face mirrored her pleasure, and yet she caught a sad pensiveness about his smile. *He's thinking of me and feeling guilty for bringing me away from all the beauty of my home,* she thought, *but I must make him know how happy I really am and how I see all the nice little extras he does for me to keep me from being lonesome and missing home.*

She prayed a quick silent prayer for help and turned to him. "Elba, you do so many lovely things for me. You are so thoughtful. I want you to know I am a very happy woman."

"Oh, pshaw," he said, looking down, "I don't do anything."

He's like a little boy, she thought, *I love that shy, littly-boy confusion when he's praised.*

"But I'm glad you're happy," he continued. He pointed to a profusion of bushes that covered a wide area, "There are more, lots more."

She lifted her eyes where he pointed and scanned the mass of rose bushes that seemed to go on and on.

"They are delightful! And just look at

them — dozens of them — hundreds."

She went from bush to bush, happy as a child in her delight of the dainty flowers.

"Here's a big one, Elba, cut this one. This one is such a deep rose color! Just look at those buds!"

Elba cut the flowers as she pointed to them and soon they had a large fragrant bouquet and slowly retraced their steps to the cabin.

"Your prairie is making me eat my words over and over again," she admitted sheepishly. "I have never seen such an abundance of flowers as here. First, the carpet of crocuses in the spring and now these roses. The prairie truly holds many surprises."

Chapter 5

Restless Days

The July days passed slowly for Alma in her eighth month of pregnancy. The heat was intolerable. It sapped her energy, made her movements slower, and the need to rest more frequent. Her body was strange to her. It wasn't really her own. It was heavy and awkward. Her sore knees ached and throbbed from the extra weight.

The work dragged on endlessly. Besides housework and hoeing in the garden she was making baby clothes to add to those of Neva's and Ralph's which she had kept. (Ralph, Alma's and Elba's son, died in infancy before the little family had moved west.)

When after a long day's work she

flopped into bed, she tossed and turned and was so uncomfortable she had trouble getting to sleep.

"I wish I were an octagonal shape," she said to Elba one night as she shifted from side to side. "I'd have more sides to turn on."

"Poor dear," he said and reached for her hand. "This last month is going to be difficult for you, especially in this heat. Wish I could help more."

"I'll survive." She gave a wry grin. "This one is different from either of the others. I seem to be more uncomfortable. Probably because it's so active."

"We'll have to be thinking of names again soon," Elba said with a yawn. "Not all that much time left."

"Can't come too soon for me," Alma sighed. "Did you talk to Mrs. Fox about being with me for the delivery?"

"Yes. She's all ready to come as soon as we give her the word."

"It will be marvellous to feel slim and light again. If it's a girl, I'd like to call her Lela."

"Lela?" Elba lifted himself on his elbow and looked at her. "Isn't that the name of the ship we went on for our honeymoon?"

"So you remembered?"

"Of course, I remember. How could I forget that perfect cruise across the Great Lakes? You were so beautiful, and I was so proud of my new bride."

"It *was* a perfect trip wasn't it? I guess there were other passengers on the ship, but I don't remember any. All I could see was my handsome husband." She laid her head on his shoulder and relived the memory of those days.

"Remember how beautiful the full moon was coming up over the water?" she asked dreamily.

"I remember, Alma, and I also remember the joy I felt as I held you in my arms and thought, she's mine! She's mine to have and to hold. Your parents kept such a close watch on us that all I ever dared were a few stolen kisses and hugs."

"Go on with you! They weren't that strict." She laughed.

"Well, *I* thought they were." He kissed her and turned on his side and plumped up his pillow. "Where'd you get the name Neva?" he asked sleepily.

"Neva is the name of a ship also. In fact The Neva and Lela are sister ships that have plied the Great Lakes for some years. I always liked those names."

"Uh-huh." He was asleep.

"I'm glad you can sleep anyway." She tried to find a comfortable position, but the straw tick was lumpy in some places and thin in others. Her back felt like she was lying on bare boards. Tears forced their way through tightly shut lids. She began to pray silently.

Dear Lord, I am glad this little one is coming, but I am so uncomfortable. I need your help and comfort now. I know you care because your Word says "For we do not have a High Priest who cannot sympathize with our weaknesses, but was in all points tempted as we are, yet without sin. "

A slight breeze stole through the window and fanned her face. A peace surrounded her and she was calmed.

Thank you, Lord Jesus, for caring. How hot and uncomfortable and agonizing it was for you on the cross. You couldn't even lie down to relax your poor aching muscles. I guess even a lumpy straw tick would have felt good to you. Thank you for suffering for my sins. Thank you for taking my place on the cross and for your wonderful, understanding love.

She slept.

Chapter 6

Elba's Shop

Having finished breaking the prairie sod for added crop the following spring, Elba was ready to start building his shop. During the winter logging operation, he had set aside some choice logs. Now he was eager to begin.

He levelled the ground on the north side of the cabin and squared it off. He honed his axe until it was almost as sharp as his razor, then he went to the pile of logs he had saved and chose four larger ones. These he placed on the ground to form a rectangle.

With his axe he made notches in the logs about one and one half feet from the end. he then lifted one of the logs lying east and west, turned it over and placed it on the north and south log so the notches matched perfectly and the log lay even with the other making a neat corner. He did the same with the other log, and soon he had the first four logs of the building in place.

He stepped back to admire his work and rest a little. He removed his cap and reached into his overall pocket for his red bandannna. He wiped the perspiration from his face and replaced his cap.

That's a neat start, he thought. *I think it will go up quite quickly.*

Alma came out of the cabin with a glass of cold tea for him. Neva was close behind.

"Elba Swayze, how do you ever manage to lift those logs by yourself? Why didn't you call me? I could help."

He accepted the glass gratefully. "Those aren't really logs, dear. More like poles. When I get up higher, I'll have to get help. But not you. You're in no shape to be lifting and climbing around. I'll go over tonight and see if young Jack Brown can come and help me. You wouldn't mind having him around for a few days?"

"Who's coming?" Neva was excited.

"Jack Brown." Elva smiled at her. "If it's all right with your mother."

"I'd be glad to have him. It's a joy

when anybody comes. But where would he sleep?"

"I'll put a couple horse blankets on some hay in the barn. The animals stay out all night anyway, so he'll have it all to himself. He won't mind."

"Is he old?" Neva asked.

"Yes, to you he's old. But you'll like him."

"You'll be happy to have a little shop of your own again, won't you?" There was understanding in Alma's eyes.

Elba smiled at her. "Sure will. There's so many things I can do when I have a forge and anvil. I'm sure I can help some of the neighbors and maybe make a dollar or two besides."

"I'll never see you then," Alma pouted. "But I'll be glad to hear the music of the anvil again. That was one thing I loved so much in Kelvin. You always seemed near when I could hear the ring of the anvil coming from the shop."

Elba's eyes were dreamy as he said, "Yep. Guess I'm a blacksmith at heart and always will be."

After supper he rode his horse four miles to the Brown homestead. Two younger girls were outside in the yard and saw him coming. They ran to the kitchen door.

"Pa, somebody's comin' ahorseback."

Bill Brown and his wife and young Jack came hurrying out of the house to welcome him.

"Hello, Elba." Bill's weatherbeaten face smiled his welcome as he caught the horse's bridle. "Come on in. Jack, take care of Elba's horse, please."

Bill introduced Elba to his wife and daughters, Doris and Sadie. Mrs. Brown was a thin pleasant-faced lady with her dark hair pulled back and wound in a tight knob.

Doris was chubby and merry with twinkly blue eyes and straw-colored hair. Sadie was dark like her mother with large serious eyes, too big for her thin face.

Elba greeted them and said, "Well, I can't stay long. I came to ask a favor. You see I'm building a log shed to house my forge and anvil and I need someone to help me for a day or two. I'd be mighty obliged if you could spare young Jack."

"I'm sure that can be arranged," Bill said.

"Come on in and at least have a cup of coffee," Mrs. Brown said graciously. "We don't see anyone all that often. Can't you stay for a while?"

48

"Yes, please do." Doris came up and took his hand and led him into the kitchen.

Elba smiled at her and said, "I have a little girl at home. Her name is Neva, but she's smaller than either of you two."

"Why didn't you bring her?"

"Well, you see," Elba said, "there wasn't room. I hope to take Jack back with me."

They sat around the kitchen table made of bare pine boards scrubbed clean and white. Mrs. Brown took the coffee pot from the stove and poured coffee into brown earthenware mugs. She set a plate of cinnamon rolls on the table.

Elba looked around the cabin. It was larger than theirs at home, but it lacked the little homey touches that Alma seemed to be able to provide and that somehow expressed her personality.

Jack came in and his father said, "Elba needs help for a couple days. Reckon you could give him a hand?"

"Sure." Jack's shy young face showed his pleasure. His mother handed him a mug of coffee. "I don't have money to offer you, but I can bring you some cordwood."

"That's fine," Bill agreed. "Can always use wood."

"How's your wife? Wish you'd brought her," Mrs. Brown said longingly. "I scarcely ever see another woman."

"She keeps quite well, thank you, but she's not stirring very far from home these days. You see, we're expecting a little one next month."

Mrs. Brown's face lit up transforming her sharp features. "Oh, really? That's nice. If there's anything I can do just let me know. I'll be glad to help."

"Thank you." Elba's grey eyes smiled his appreciation. "That's kind of you. I'll tell Alma."

Jack got a few things together to take with him. Elba mounted the horse, and Jack jumped up behind, holding his bundle.

"Good-bye, Elba."

"Good-bye, Jack. Be good."

Jack grinned and waved.

"Good-bye, Mr. Swayze," the little girls called.

Elba said good-bye to all of them as he and Jack started down the drive.

Mrs. Brown called after him, "When the baby is a little older, tell your wife to come and see me."

"Will do."

As they rode along, Elba tried to strike up a conversation, but Jack was shy and answered only in monosyllables. Eventually Elba gave up and started to sing. Jack forgot himself and whistled the accompaniment.

"You like music, I take it."

"Sure do, but we don't have any kind of instrument at home. I go to the square dances just to hear the music."

"You mean you don't dance with all those pretty girls?" He turned and looked at Jack and saw him blush.

"Naw. I'm too shy. They'd laugh at me."

"A nice looking young fellow like you? They won't laugh. They'd be proud you asked them." He paused a moment then continued, "You'll get over your shyness some day."

"Maybe." Jack didn't sound too sure.

In the days to come Jack and Elba worked hard, and soon the shed was finished. They chinked the walls and roof and since Elba didn't have proper doors and windows, they were made from boards and fastened on with rawhide hinges. The forge and anvil were carried in and leveled on the dirt floor.

"When I bank up the house for winter, I'll bank up the shop too, and it will be snug to work in." Elba was pleased with their work.

"Now, let's load the wagon up with some cordwood and I'll take you home. I sure appreciate your help."

"Aw, that's nothing. I enjoyed it."

Alma gave Jack a crocheted doily to give his mother, and Neva had a tiny cake to give his sisters.

"Tell your mother I plan to come and visit her," Alma told Jack.

"She'll be glad," Jack called back. "She's terrible lonely."

"I wish he didn't have to go. I like Jack," Neva said sadly.

"I like him too," Alma said, "but he never talks much."

"He talks to me, lots," Neva nodded her head decidedly.

Chapter 7

Sewing Machine

On a hot Saturday morning early in August, Elba came in from doing the chores. He placed the milk bucket on the kitchen cabinet and stood looking at Alma. She was sitting in her chair taking tiny stitches on a small white garment. Occasionally, she laid the sewing in her lap and used her fan to cool her flushed face.

"How are you feeling this morning, dear?" Elba gazed intently at her as he wiped his forehead with his red bandanna.

Alma looked up and smiled. "Oh, I'm all right. It's just this heat that bothers me." She got up to care for the milk.

"There's an auction sale over at

Smith's homestead. I thought I'd go and see if there's anything we need that I could get at a good price."

"Another family going broke?" Alma asked concerned.

"Yes. Says he can't make a go of it, and his wife wants her children to grow up in Ontario."

Elba sighed and ran his fingers through his hair. "Do you feel up to coming with me? We wouldn't have to stay long."

Alma smiled wistfully. "You go, dear. I'd just rather stay put these days. Can't face the heat and the ride."

Elba's grey eyes spoke his concern. "You sure you'll be all right? What if Baby should decide to come?"

Alma held out her hand and Elba took it in his big capable one. "I'll be just fine," she said. "It should be another week or so before Baby comes."

"You sure now? I don't want to leave you if you are anxious at all."

"I'm fine," she said and lifted her face for his kiss. He took her upturned face in his hands and kissed her. "I never like to leave you, but these days I mind it more than ever because I worry about you when I'm gone."

She chuckled. "I'm supposed to be the

worrier in this family. Now be off with you." She waved him off as he put on his cap and went out the door.

Neva, playing in the shade with Girl beside her, ran to Elba when she saw him getting the team ready.

"Where ya going, Papa? Can I go?"

Papa looked down at her and rumpled her curls. "I want you to stay and look after Mama today. You can run errands for her or get her a nice cool drink of water from the well. I won't be gone long."

Neva was disappointed. She loved to go with Papa, but she also felt important because he had asked her to care for Mama. She watched Papa drive away then ran to the house. She stood with her hands on the arm of Mama's chair.

"Papa said I had to look after you, Mama. Do you want anything?"

Alma smiled and placed her hands over Neva's "I'm glad I have you to take care of me," she said. "I can't think of anything I need right now, but if I do I'll call you."

"Maybe a cold drink from the well?"

"Come to think of it, dear, that would be lovely."

Neva beamed her pleasure. She picked up the water bucket and lifted the dipper out, placing it on the table.

"Should I throw out the old water?"

"Pour it on the rosebush, please."

Soon Neva was back with a half bucket of fresh cool water. She poured a glass and gave it to Alma.

"Here, Mama."

Alma took the glass gratefully. She noticed the water had splashed on Neva's dress and legs, but she made no reference to it.

"That's good! Just what I needed. Why don't you have some too. It's so cold."

"I *know* — I pumped all the warm water out."

As Neva wandered off to play again she said, "Call me if you need me."

"Thank you, Neva. I will."

What a dear little thing she is, Alma thought. *She's thoughtful like her father. I am a very happy, blessed woman.* She daydreamed as she continued to work on the baby kimono she was making.

She remembered a little more than four years ago when she had been waiting for Neva, her first. How happy she had been and yet apprehensive as the time drew near. Then two years later little Ralph had been born. He had died when he was just five days under a year. He would be talking and running all around by now if he had lived.

Tears welled up in her eyes and the old familiar ache came to her heart. *I guess one never gets over it,* she thought. *The hurt and emptiness will always be there.* "Yes, Ralph," she said aloud, "my little boy, you have your own place in my heart. I'll always love your memory. Some day in heaven I'll see you again. I'll have you again." She wiped her eyes. *I wonder what heaven is like,* she mused. *Will Ralph be a baby still or will he have grown? Will I know him? Will he really belong to me?*

Tears flowed again and she prayed "Dear Lord Jesus, there's so much I don't understand about Your heaven and what it will be like. I know it will be beautiful, and there will be no more tears or pain or sin. Best of all You will be there. It will be so wonderful to see You — Your lovely face and Your hands with the nail scars in them. I love You and I worship You."

She looked at the clock on the lamp shelf and decided it was time to prepare lunch. She struggled to her feet, pushing hard with her hands on the arms of the chair. *I'm like an old woman,* she thought and giggled. She patted her tummy and said, "It won't be long now until you'll be

57

free and I'll be free. Glorious thought!"

Lunch was about ready when Neva's voice came to her through the open door.

"Papa's comin'!"

Alma's heart gave its accustomed leap of gladness, and she sang as she finished setting the table. She heard the team and wagon draw up to the door. "Wonder what he got?" She went outside to see.

Neva was already clambering into the wagon.

"What didya get, Papa?"

"Here's something for you to help Mama with the washing."

He handed her a thing with a handle like a broom only shorter and at one end was a metal cone with holes on it.

"What is it?" Neva was examining it closely.

"It's a clothes plunger. When Mama has the clothes soaking in soapy water in the tub, you plunge this thing up and down and the suction takes the dirt out."

Neva was down in a jiffy showing Mama.

"Look what Papa bought me."

"Well, I declare," Alma said taking the plunger in her hands. "What'll they think of next? This is great, Elba. Thanks."

Elba was grinning his loveable grin

58

as he dragged something heavy to the back of the wagon. "I got something for you too, Alma. Something you'll like."

"What is it?" Alma was as excited as Neva.

Elba opened the tailgate and lifted down a treadle sewing machine.

Alma clapped her hands. "Oh, Elba, a sewing machine! I'm so glad. I've missed my machine so much." She threw her arms around his neck. "Thank you."

"Glad I could do it. I hated to see you doing all the sewing by hand. I knew you missed your machine even though you didn't complain."

Alma ran her fingers over the smooth finish of the wood. Her eyes were shining.

"It's just beautiful!"

Elba took it inside and lifted the cover off. There was the machine head with the brand name "White" on the side, the thread spindle, the shiny foot and needle and the sliding door over the bobbin.

"It's a good make," Elba said, "and it's nearly new."

Alma opened the sliding door and saw the bobbin already full of white thread. "Mrs. Smith must have been using the machine right up to the last. I'm sure it was hard for her to give it up, poor woman."

Elba slipped the belt in place while Alma found a spool of white thread and a pillow case that needed hemming. Elba enjoyed watching her as she threaded the machine.

"Bring me a chair, Neva, please," she said, when she was ready to try out the machine.

"Here, Mama." Neva shoved the chair up behind Alma. As Alma sat down she placed the bottom of the pillow case under the shiny foot and put her feet on the iron treadle and said, "Here goes."

The machine whirred busily away. Alma guided the hem of the pillow case, and beautiful even stitches were formed so fast one could scarcely see them being made.

Halfway around the hem, Alma stopped to examine the work and to rest her sore knee. (Her knee had hurt her for years as a result of a serious fall. She usually walked with the aid of a cane.)

"Does it bother your knee to work it, dear?" Elba asked.

"Just a little, but I'll get used to it. Isn't it wonderful. Here I've done in a few minutes what would take a half hour to do by hand. Oh, Elba, perhaps later I can get some sewing to do for the neighbors and earn a bit of money for us."

"Well, I didn't buy it for that. I bought it for you."

"I know you did, dear, but I'd love to help out too." She patted his hand. "Well, I better finish this."

"Would you like to help Mama sew, Neva?" Elba asked.

Neva looked at Papa half-hoping, half-doubting. "I can't. I don't know how."

"Sure you can. I'll show you." He took Neva behind the machine and said. "See this arm? It goes up and down when Mama makes the treadle go. You sit down here on the floor, and when Mama gets the machine started you can work it by pushing this arm up and down."

Neva's eager face was full of smiles.

"I can do that. Will that make it sew?"

"Sure will," Elba said and winked at her. "You and Mama will be partners, the best sewers in the country."

Alma turned the fly wheel and said, "All right, Neva, just make it go evenly, not too fast."

Neva pushed and pulled, at first a bit jerkily but Alma helped with the treadle until Neva got the rhythm.

The hem was soon finished, and they all marvelled at the neat, even stitches.

"Let's sew more, Mama, more."

Alma laughed. "Not today, dear, but I'm sure glad I have a partner, and you can help me lots of times."

"It's easy to sew," Neva said more to herself than anyone as she went outside to find her dog. "I can sew, Girl. I can sew!"

Chapter 8

Baby Sister

August 9, 1906 was a hot sweltering day. Neva came downstairs expecting to find Mama making her breakfast as usual. Instead, she found Bertha, the neighbor girl, in the kitchen. Neva liked Bertha. Even though she was a big girl, she always talked to Neva and was kind to her.

"Come and eat your breakfast, Neva," Bertha said. Somehow Neva didn't feel like eating. Things seemed different. She missed Mama. However, she tried to eat as Bertha fussed over her.

Neva heard someone upstairs talking to Mama. "Who's up there?" she asked, with her mouth full of toast.

"That's my mother," Bertha replied.

"She's helping your mother."

Helping Mama, Neva thought. *What help does Mama need? She's the one who always helps everyone else.* She noticed Bertha put the kettle on and thought, *She doesn't know much. It's far too early to get lunch. She doesn't know how Mama does things.* Bertha and her mother were climbing upstairs and down frequently. Neva couldn't understand it all. Things were topsy-turvy today.

Girl was playing outside, going round and round in circles chasing her tail. As Neva went out to play, Girl bounded up, tail wagging, and gave Neva a big slurp on her cheek. Neva tossed a stick and commanded, "Fetch, Girl, fetch." Girl raced after the stick and skidded to a stop in the gravel. She almost knocked Neva over as she brought the stick back.

"Be careful, Girl, you're getting so big."

She saw the calf down by the barn in its pen. "Let's go see the calf." She and Girl ran together. Neva tried to get the calf to come to her at the fence, but Girl excitedly began to chase the calf around the pen. Neva scolded her telling her again and again to stop, but it had no effect. She was almost in tears when Bertha heard the racket and came to the door.

"Neva, come away from the calf."

"Girl won't listen."

"If you come, she'll follow you."

Neva ran to the house calling Girl, and soon Girl was running along behind her. Tired of playing with the dog, Neva decided to go and see Mama. Maybe Mama was sick. Maybe she needed Neva to help her right now. She rushed into the house. "I'm going up to see Mama." She started up the ladder.

"No, dear, not just now. Wait a little while. Would you like a glass of milk and some cookies?"

Neva was puzzled. She didn't want to wait, and she didn't want any milk. She just wanted to see her own dear Mama. She sat in the corner by the wood box. "I don't like you," she said under her breath. "Why can't I see her? She's my mama and she prob'ly needs me. But I'm not going to cry. I'm not going to let Bertha see me cry."

Then she heard a strange noise upstairs — like a cat or something — maybe like a baby lamb crying. "What's that?"

"What's what?" asked Bertha.

"That noise like a baby lamb or something."

"That's a baby all right, but not a baby lamb."

Now whose baby could it be? Neva's eyes got big. She looked at Bertha and asked, "Whose baby is it?"

Bertha picked her up and swung her around the kitchen. "It's your mother's baby. Isn't that great?"

"Did your mother bring a baby for Mama?" Neva could hardly believe what Bertha was saying.

"Something like that," Bertha said and laughed. "You just be patient for a little while longer and you can see the baby."

Neva wanted to ask a lot of questions, but she thought she'd wait and ask Mama. She sat quietly in the corner hugging herself, trying to take it all in. She felt warm and happy. *Now I won't be alone,* she thought, *I'll have someone to play with. I like playing with Girl but she can't talk.*

A while later Bertha announced, "Come on, we can go up and see the baby now." Bertha took Neva'a hand, but Neva couldn't wait. She leaped up the ladder and ran to Mama's room. Then she stopped short. Sure enough, there was Mama in bed, and beside her was a little bundle wrapped in a warm blanket. All of a sudden Neva felt shy.

"Neva dear, come and see Mama," Alma held out her arms. Neva snuggled up against Mama. She looked at the tiny bundle. Mama said, "This is our new baby. This is your own baby sister. We're going to name her Lela." Mama pulled the blanket off the baby.

"It's so little," Neva said in a small voice. "Will she be able to play with me?"

"Not right at first, but when she grows a bit she will." Neva looked wonderingly at the little pink face and the tiny folded hands. She touched one little hand and Baby took hold of her finger. "Look Mama, what's she doing? She's holding my finger tight."

"Oh, I guess she's telling you she likes you and never wants you to go away."

"Tell her I won't go away, Mama. I'll be right here."

"Thank you, dear. I'm going to need your help a lot. You'll be able to run errands for me and bring me things I need. You'll have to help me look after your sister."

Neva felt happy inside as she thought about being Mama's helper. She was so glad to have a new baby sister all her own.

When Papa came in with the milk

pail and set it down on the table, Neva asked him, her eyes sparkling, "Guess what, Papa. We got a baby!"

"You don't say?" Elba pretended surprise. "Now what kind of baby is it? A kitten?" Neva laughed and shook her head.

"Oh, I know, it's a baby calf." Papa puckered his brow and Neva knew he was teasing.

"Not a calf."

"Well, what then, a puppy?"

"Oh, Papa, you know it's our baby, a baby girl."

Elba caught her up and hugged her. "Yeah, I know, Kitten, and I'm so glad. But we'll both have to help Mama a lot."

"I know. She already told me."

They went together to Alma's bed. Elba knelt down beside her and stroked her hair. "How's my prairie rose?" he asked softly. He took the baby in his arms and cuddled her. With his cheek against her forehead he said, "And you're my little rosebud."

A few days later when Mama was up again and the neighbors had returned home, Mama said, "Come Neva, you can help me bathe the baby." Neva stood on a chair beside the table and watched as Mama took off all Baby's clothes. Neva loved Baby's clothes. Neva loved Baby's tiny pink feet. Baby kicked and kicked with her feet in the dishpan of water. Neva laughed. Then Baby splashed water on the table and some went on Neva.

"Mama, Baby splashed water on me," she said in surprise.

Mama laughed. "She didn't mean to, Neva. She just enjoys kicking the water with her feet. Bring me the talcum powder from the dresser, please."

When Baby was all powdered and dressed in clean clothes, Mama said, "You go sit in Papa's chair, and I'll let you hold your sister while I clean up here."

Happiness flooded her heart. She sat so very still and held baby so carefully. Baby felt tiny in her arms, but cuddly and soft. "I'll always take care of you, Lela. I won't let Girl hurt you 'cause she doesn't know that you're just new." She put her nose down to Baby's head. Baby smelled so clean and sweet like a new-born puppy's breath — only nicer.

I wonder if she would like me to sing to her like Mama sings to me, Neva wondered. She rocked back and forth and sang:

> Up, up in the sky,
> The little birds fly.

Baby wiggled and flopped her little arms. "Look, Mama, Baby is doing the motions."

"I guess she likes your singing. Perhaps she will go to sleep."

Neva continued:

Down, down in their nests
The little birds rest.
With a wing on the left
And a wing on the right
The dear little birdies
Sleep all the long night.

Baby yawned and popped her thumb in her mouth and drifted off to sleep.

Chapter 9

Runaway

Neva, who was playing with little Sister on a blanket on the floor, heard Mama say, "Elba, will you hitch up Nettie for me, please? We're having a quilting bee at Cudmores' today."

"Sure, dear, I'll leave her tied near the house. It will be good for you to get away and be with other women for a change." His kind grey eyes showed understanding as he smiled at Mama.

Neva jumped up and down, clapping her hands, "Are we going, too?"

"Of course, you and the baby are going. You'll have fun with the other children." Mama took Neva's little face in her hands and bent down to touch noses. "You are always helping Papa drive the horses. I couldn't get along without you."

"Good-e-e-e," Neva danced around the kitchen until she was out of breath.

"You mind Sister while I finish the work and get ready." Mama laughed at Neva's antics as she continued to wash the dishes.

Oh, dear, that's going to take a long time, Neva thought, but leaning up close to Sister's face, she asked her, "Do you want to go for a buggy ride and see lots of kids?"

Sister only grinned and gurgled and grabbed one of Neva's thick brown curls.

"You always pull my hair!" Neva said disgustedly, loosening Sister's little fingers. Baby only smiled and grabbed for something else.

"I can't wait till you can talk and play with me. Mama says it won't be long, but I think it's long."

Neva couldn't stay still. She could hardly wait. Every few minutes she ran to see if Mama was ready to go yet. "Can I help?"

"No, dear. Just look after Sister. I won't be long."

"Won't be long, won't be long," Neva sang as she hopped around. "Why do grown-ups always say that?" she wondered.

72

Two or three minutes later, Neva was back at the bedroom door, standing on one foot then the other.

"What have we here?" Mama asked, chuckling, "a little stork?"

Mama looks pretty in her second-best dress, Neva thought, as Mama, face flushed from hurrying, pinned her wide hat over her soft brown hair.

Mama smiled at Neva in the mirror. "Run and fetch my sewing basket, and we'll be on our way."

"I've got the basket," Neva sang, slamming the screen door behind her as she ran to the buggy. "You are going to take us for a nice ride today, Nettie," she said as she climbed into the buggy and placed the basket under the seat. Mama put little Sister down beside her, then untied Nettie. As Mama was climbing into the buggy with one foot up on the high step, Nettie, seeing the pasture gate open decided she would rather eat some nice sweet grass than travel weary miles over a dusty trail. Suddenly she swung to the left and headed for the gate.

As the wheel was jerked forward, it banged into Mama and knocked her down. Baby rolled over on the seat and started to howl.

Neva felt her mouth go dry. Something seemed to be grabbing at her throat; she could hardly breathe. Her heart was fluttering against her ribs like a little wild canary in a cage.

She knelt on the floor of the buggy and put one arm around Sister to keep her from falling off the seat. Neva was used to helping Papa drive, but never alone. She saw that one rein had fallen and was dragging uselessly along the ground. She grabbed the one remaining rein and yanked with all her might.

Nettie was surprised to have her head pulled suddenly to the left. She swerved and cramped the left front buggy wheel under the body. The buggy lifted and teetered precariously. Neva was knocked against the seat and Baby almost fell off, but Neva held her tight. Tears were streaming down Neva's face. *We're going to tip over. We'll be killed. What do I do now?*

Suddenly Nettie stopped just before she ran into the barbwire fence. Neva jumped to her feet and looked back to see if Mama were badly hurt. There she was coming, running as fast as she could with the cane which she had picked up where she fell.

"Hold on, Neva, Mama's coming."

I hope Mama's lame knee wasn't hurt

so she'll have to walk on crutches again,
Neva thought.

Mama spoke quietly to Nettie and placed the fallen rein over the dashboard. She took Nettie by the bridle and straightened the buggy out. Then she got in the buggy and quieted the girls. Soon they were on their way again.

After they had settled down and Nettie's hooves were beating out the familiar, rhythmic 'clip-clop,' Mama said, "You are a very brave little girl, Neva. I don't know what might have happened if you hadn't been there. I was praying that Jesus would help you and show you what to do and He did. It could have been very different, but thanks to you we are all safe." She smiled at Neva and there were tears in her eyes. "Papa is going to be very proud of you when I tell him."

Neva looked up at Mama in surprise. Her little face lit up with pleasure at Mama's praise. She didn't know how she had been brave or exactly what brave meant, but it felt good to know Mama was pleased with her.

Chapter 10

Quilting Bee

Nettie trotted evenly up the lane to the Cudmore home, very docile now as though to recompense for her earlier misdemeanor. Several horse and buggy rigs were tied to the fence, and ladies with large hats and long, full skirts were gathering up their sewing baskets and entering the house.

"Lookit the big house!" Neva exclaimed in astonishment.

"It certainly is that!" Alma replied as she gazed at the large, double-story log house, neatly plastered and painted white.

"I wonder how many rooms there are." Alma was mentally comparing it with their house with only one room downstairs.

She drove Nettie alongside the other rigs and tied her securely to the fence. Neva took the basket, and Alma carried the baby as they went into the house.

The erected quilt frame occupied the center of the large attractive room. One of the children was placing chairs around the frame.

Harriet Cudmore, a large woman with a pleasant face crowned with an abundance of red hair, came forward to greet them graciously. With outstretched arms she said, "Welcome to our home. So glad you could come, Alma." Her voice, clear and musical, still retained its clipped, precise English accent.

"Thank you, Harriet. You certainly have a comfortable, large home," Alma replied taking it all in.

Harriet chuckled. "I can't complain, but a family the size of ours requires a large house. I'll show you through it before you go home, if you wish."

"I'd like that very much," Alma smiled.

"Ladies," Harriet raised her voice to be heard above the chatter, "here's Alma with the new baby."

Everyone gathered around to greet Alma and admire the baby.

"Oh, isn't it cute!"

"Is it a girl?"

"What's her name?"

"Look at her smile in her sleep!"

"Oh, that's only a gas bubble."

The baby only stretched and yawned and settled down to continue her nap.

Harriet called to her eighteen year old daughter. "Clara, show Alma into the spare room to remove her hat and make the baby comfortable on the bed." Then she turned to Neva.

"How old are you, Neva?"

"I'm past four."

"Well, here's my little girl, Myrtle. She's six. She'll take you up to the girls' room where the other children are." The two went off happily together to play with the others.

Soon the ladies were all seated around the quilt frame, their fingers flying as they made dainty stitches along the pattern lines and their tongues flying just as fast as they chatted about all the local news of the community.

"Did you know that Mrs. Millar has a new hired girl?"

"I heard that the Brown girl is getting married."

"That so? Who's she marrying?"

"Don't know. Some fellow from over south of town."

"Bob Green fell out of the hayloft the other day and broke his leg."

"I hear the Taylors are building a new barn."

Mary Fox was examining the quilt. "Is this wool you're using for the filling, Harriet?"

"It is wool, and I carded it all myself," Harriet replied proudly.

"How do you card it?" Alma asked. "I've never seen wool carded."

"You haven't? Well, I'll show you." Harriet went into another room and returned with the carders and some sheep's wool. The carders were two oblongs of wood about ten inches by five inches with a handle at the center of the long side. On one side of the carder points of tacks or small nails protruded.

Harriet held the handle of one carder in her left hand, the oblong part toward her. On this she placed the piece of wool. The other carder she held in her right hand, the oblong away from her. Repeatedly she pulled the right hand carder over the wool on the left carder until the wool was light and fluffy.

"That's all there is to it," Harriet said smiling.

Elba could easily make me a pair of those, Alma thought.

"Doesn't it take forever?" someone asked.

"It goes quite quickly," Harriet assured them. "It all depends on how many seeds and burrs are left in after the washing process."

"Whew," another added, "what a lot of work!"

"Not as much work as spinning yarn," Alma said. "I've seen my mother sit hours and hours spinning wool or cotton into skeins."

Mary spoke up. "We really are fortunate in these days. We can just go to a store and buy all the skeins we need."

"Yes, indeed, we have things so much easier today than our mothers and grandmothers had."

"Just think, after they had spun all that yarn, they still had to weave it into cloth and then make it into garments for the family, all by hand."

"How did they ever find time to do it with all the other work? I can't find time to get my sewing down even with a machine."

"Yes, and they did so much by candlelight. I'm sure glad we have these coal-oil lamps. They give such a bright light."

"Remember they even had to *make*

their own candles too."

"You know, with all the labor-saving devices we have today, we must have lots more time than they did, and yet I seem to keep busy all the time anyway."

"So do I. I've got a pile of ironing and mending at home this high."

So it went for most of the afternoon, just light, happy chatter that brought the ladies up-to-date on local events. Finally the last stitch was in, and the beautiful quilt was finished except for the binding.

It was taken off the frame, and Harriet held it up for all to admire. It was the wedding ring pattern with interlocking wedding rings in stark white scattered over the quilt contrasting boldly against the background of variegated blues.

"Thank you, ladies. You have done a superior job. I plan to present this quilt to our new pastor at the dedication of the church in October." She folded up the quilt. "Now let us retire to the dining room for refreshments."

After they had enjoyed coffee with fresh cream and delicious cinnamon buns, Harriet said, "Now, before we disband let us read and pray." She reached for the Bible and turned to Ephesians 3:14-19 and read:

For this cause I bow my knees
unto the Father of our Lord Jesus
Christ,
Of whom the whole family in
heaven and earth is named,
That he would grant you, according to the riches of his glory, to be
strengthened with might by his
Spirit in the inner man;
That Christ may dwell in your
hearts by faith; that ye, being
rooted and grounded in love,
May be able to comprehend with
all saints what is the breadth, and
length, and depth, and height;
And to know the love of Christ,
which passeth knowledge, that ye
might be filled with all the
fullness of God.

"This, dear sisters in Christ, is Paul's
prayer and desire, not only for the
Christians in Ephesus, but for us today.

"Doesn't it encourage your heart to
know that the great apostle Paul prayed
for you and me? And such a prayer!

"He is asking God that out of the
wealth of his glory he will give us power
through the Holy Spirit to be strong in
our inner selves.

"Then he asks Christ to make his
home in our hearts by faith and that we

may have our roots and foundation in love, so that you and I together with all God's people may know how broad and long, how high and how deep Christ's love is. Even though it can never be fully known. He wants us to be completely filled with the very nature of God.

"I find this very inspiring and I do want to be receptive and obedient that I might experience the tremendous dimensions of this love that can fill our lives and natures.

"Alma, would you lead us in prayer, please?"

There was a scraping of chairs as each one knelt humbly. Alma prayed, "Dear Lord Jesus, we wait before you in praise and adoration. We thank you for your wonderful love and for what we do know and enjoy of it. But, as we heard your Word today, we do want to learn more and more of it and to truly be filled with the very nature of God.

"Now, as we leave to go to our homes, may we go with your blessing and protection.

"In Jesus' name we pray. Amen."

Chapter 11

Family Altar

The hot summer days were making the vegetables in the garden jump ahead until it seemed everything was ripening at once — peas, beans, corn, cucumbers. Alma and Neva spent most of their time in picking and canning. Alma felt very gratified as she saw the shelves in the cellar filling up with shiny jars of canned vegetables.

"Elba, next time you go to town, I need more jars," Alma said one morning at breakfast. "Try to get those mason jars with the spring tops. I like them."

"I can go today, if you need them." Elba finished his coffee and reached for the Bible as was his custom after breakfast. "I need some supplies from the hardware and blacksmith shop. Might as well go in and get them."

Elba went to the door to call Neva who was playing with Girl. "Prayer time, Neva."

"Can I sit here on the doorstep with Girl? I'll listen." She looked up eagerly.

Elba smiled. "W-e-e-ll," he drawled, "we aren't very many. We really need you to help us sing, and we just like to look at your face rather than your back."

Neva always responded happily to a need. She came back to her place at the table.

Elba sat down at his place at the head of the table. "Alma, will you lead us in a hymn?"

Alma's clear voice led and was joined by Neva's treble and Elba's deep bass as they sang the simple yet profound lyrics of "What a Friend We Have in Jesus."

Then Elba read from Colossians 3:1-4:

If ye then be risen with Christ, seek those things which are above, where Christ sitteth on the right hand of God.

Set your affection on things above, not on things on the earth.

For ye are dead and your life is hid with Christ in God.

When Christ who is your life, shall

appear, then shall ye also appear with Him in glory.

They knelt in prayer. In the quiet time of worship, a peace stole into their hearts, and God's strength renewed their spirits.

"I get a lot of help from our family prayer time," Alma said as she cleared up the table. "It prepares me for the busy day."

"Yep. It sure does," Elba said, getting up and shoving his chair in. "We're so busy that unless we keep this special time to worship God, we could go all day and never find time."

"We do need to have our thoughts lifted up to heavenly things as we read each morning. I need to be reminded that there are more important things than just cooking meals and washing clothes and canning tomatoes," Alma finished with a giggle. She was standing at the table with a pile of dirty dishes in her hands. She looked at Elba and there was a glow, an inner beauty, that radiated from her face.

He walked over to her and taking the dishes from her hands put them on the table. He took her in his arms. "My little preacher," he said and laid his cheek against her hair. "I do try to focus my attention on things above, but it seems that so much of our time here on this earth is taken up just looking after our physical needs. It keeps me on the jump getting enough food for us to eat and clothes to wear and fuel to keep us warm."

"I know, dear." Alma snuggled close in his arms — they were such a haven of comfort. She felt so secure, so loved. "We really do work hard, but I suppose that's the way it has to be. I think the secret is to live in His presence, to let our hearts worship and go out to Him even while we are busy. I'm going to try to meditate more on the Word and lift my heart in praise while I am washing dishes or ironing or whatever."

"I do that a lot when I'm riding the binder or driving to town. Sometimes I talk right out loud, and the Lord and I have a good time of fellowship together," Elba finished with a smile.

"Well, don't you think that is what Paul meant?" she asked with shining eyes. "He realized we would always be surrounded by earthly things and that our physical needs would always have to be met, but while we are doing that we can keep the Lord first in our lives."

"No doubt," Elba answered thoughtfully. "Paul probably learned that secret when he was sewing tents — Man! What a job! I'm sure glad I'm a blacksmith or a farmer rather than a tentmaker."

Alma giggled. "I can't picture you, with all your energy, sitting there sewing tents."

A protest from the baby's crib interrupted them.

"Oh, dear! I better look after Lela. She's probably hungry." Alma hurried over to the crib in the corner.

"And I better get off to town if I expect to get anything done today." He went out to get the team.

Chapter 12

Visitors

On a bright fall day when Alma's hands were stained red from making beet pickles, she heard a horse and buggy drive into the yard.

"Neva, would you go and see who that is while I try to get this mess off my hands."

Neva dashed out the door, but instead of welcoming the visitors as Alma expected, she took one look and dashed back inside. "It's Mrs. Cudmore and a girl."

"Well, why didn't you invite them in?"

"I will! You said see who it is."

Alma snickered. "That's right, I did. I'll have to be more explicit," she said to the empty room because Neva was back outside again.

When her hands were somewhat clean, Alma hurried to the door. Neva was coming with Mrs. Cudmore and Lillie, the oldest girl, close behind.

"Harriet, what a happy surprise!" Alma stretched out her arms in welcome. "So glad to see you. How are you?"

She turned to Lillie with a smile.

"How nice of you to come to see us. Come in. Come in."

Alma was keenly aware of her small one-room downstairs as she recalled the large Cudmore home. However, she knew that to motherly Mrs. Cudmore, gracious hospitality would mean more than luxurious surroundings.

"Let me take your hats and shawls. Please excuse the looks of the kitchen. I'm in the middle of making beet pickles." She placed the wraps on the end of the couch and went to the kitchen cabinet for cups. "The kettle is humming on the back of the stove, so we'll have a cup of tea just now."

Lillie walked over to the crib. "My, the baby has grown since you were at our place for the quilting bee. See, Mother, isn't she a plump little dear?"

As she looked at the baby, Mrs. Cudmore exclaimed, "She has grown! She

92

looks healthy, Alma. Is she a good baby?"

"Yes, generally speaking, she's a happy little soul. Neva is a great help in caring for her and also in helping me around the house."

Neva, who wasn't used to strangers making a fuss over her baby, felt warm and happy at mother's praise.

"Where's Myrtle?" she asked Mrs. Cudmore.

"She's at school with the others."

"Wish I could go to school," Neva pouted.

"You'll go when you're old enough," Mrs. Cudmore assured her. "They grow up so quickly. First, it's the break when they go off to school, and before you know it they're finished and interested in some boy or girl who wants to take them away from home." She looked at Lillie who blushed and turned her head away.

"I'm never going to go away from my mama," Neva asserted.

They all smiled and Alma wondered if Lillie were soon to be "taken away." She cleared an end of the table to make room for cups and saucers, milk and fresh cream, and a plate of cookies. She poured a glass of milk for Neva.

"Pull your chairs up, ladies, and we'll have a cup of tea."

"I suppose with all your help at home, Harriet, you have your canning and pickling all done?"

"Most of it," Harriet agreed. "Still have our sauerkraut to do. But that is one reason why we came. It looks like you need some help.

"I sure could use some help, but we can't afford to pay anyone," Alma said sadly.

"I hear that you are a seamstress."

"Yes, I am. Do you need some sewing done?"

"Lillie, here, needs some dresses made. We have the material." She rummaged in her carrying bag and took out several lengths of yardage.

"Oh, where did you get such pretty fabric?" Alma fingered the cloth lovingly.

"My mother sent it from Ontario," Harriet said.

"They have such pretty prints at home, don't they? Wish we could get stuff like this here."

Harriet hesitated, then continued, "If you would make the dresses, we wondered if Lillie could work for you in order to pay for your work."

Alma's face lit up. "That would be wonderful! I love to sew, and I'll be glad for some help right now."

"Then it's all settled," Mrs. Cudmore smiled, "and everyone's happy."

Lillie's face was a picture of happiness. "I'll be glad to work for you, Mrs. Swayze."

"It will be nice to have you here especially for the fittings. It usually is a problem to have people come for fittings. This way you'll be right here."

"I can hardly wait to see what the dresses will be like," Lillie said.

Alma hesitated. "The only trouble is, we don't have a guest room."

"That doesn't matter," Lillie broke in. "I can stay at home and ride back and forth as long as the weather is nice. I could sleep here on the couch if it is raining, couldn't I?"

"Sure. If you don't mind, I'll be glad to have you."

"Then we'll plan on Lillie being here tomorrow morning." Mrs. Cudmore smiled happily and sipped her tea.

Lela awakened and Lillie went over to get her. "Where are the diapers, Neva?"

Neva brought a clean diaper and stood overseeing the process. "Mama puts powder on," she said and brought the powder tin.

Lillie changed the diaper, found a blanket for the baby and they wandered

outside, Neva and Girl close beside them.
Alma and Harriet settled down for a cozy
chat.

"Were you raised around here, Harriet?"

"No, Alma, my folks came from
England and settled in Ontario, near
Exeter."

"That so? I was raised around Tillsonburg."

"We were married," Harriet continued, "when I was twenty. Henry had
taken a homestead 100 miles from
Emerson, Manitoba. We came by train
and team and settled near Crystal City."

"Did you have a home to come to?"

"No, we lived with a brother until we
got a log house built. For the first whole
summer we lived in it we only had a dirt
floor."

"You've had your hardships too,
haven't you? Did you get lonsome at first
for home and all you had left in
Ontario?" There was longing in Alma's
voice.

"I sure did. I cried myself to sleep
many times. I didn't get back home to see
my folks for ten years. I had six children
by then."

"I hope it isn't ten years before I get
to see my parents and family again, but

with money as scarce as it is, I may never get there." Tears came to Alma's eyes as she thought of that possibility.

"Cheer up, Alma. Things got better for us. I'm sure they will for you, too." Harriet patted Alma's hand.

"When did you move to Cannington-Manor, then?"

Harriet looked out the window as though remembering that trip. "We came here in 1902. We had ten children then and Mr. Doney, the preacher, boarded with us and we also had a hired man," she finished with a laugh.

"What a houseful!" Alma said shaking her head.

"Yes, but you know, the older ones look after the younger ones and they all have their chores to do, so one more doesn't matter."

Lillie and Neva came back with the baby, and Alma and Lillie discussed styles for the dresses.

"I don't have any patterns and I don't know where to get them," Lillie said.

"That's no problem," Alma assured her, "if you know how you want them made. When I had my training I learned how to measure and make my own patterns. Just describe how you want them, and I can go from there."

Lillie asked for the mail order catalogue, and they poured over that until finally Lillie chose the styles she wanted.

With the tape measure, Alma took measurements of bust, waist, hips, length of bodice, length of sleeve and length of skirt. She wrote them all down in a little book.

"Do you have any old newspapers at your place? I can cut the patterns from them."

"Yes, lots of them. I can bring a pile when I come to work tomorrow."

Goodbyes were said. Alma, with a new lift in her heart and a lilt in her voice, went back to her work of finishing the pickling.

Chapter 13

Fall Rush

With Lillie's help the canning went forward at a good pace. Crocks of sauerkraut were lined up beside jars of dill pickles, nine-day pickles, and bread-and-butter pickles. Bottles of red chili sauce and green relish gave the shelves a Christmasy festive look.

Elba complained that he was afraid to come to the house lest he get pickled also.

In between times Alma cut the patterns and sewed on Lillie's dresses. Periodically there had to be a fitting. Lillie's pretty face was flushed with joy and anticipation as Alma exclaimed how pretty she would look in her new dresses.

1906 went down in history as the year of the big crop. Some people harvested forty bushels per acre. Elba's crop was fair. The nearest elevator was eighteen miles away so much time was spent in hauling grain.

Elba also kept busy hauling wheat to the grist mill to be ground into flour, filling the root cellar with turnips, potatoes, beets, and parsnips, and banking up the house and shop and stable.

With much of Alma's time taken up with the baby and with everyone so busy, Neva began to feel neglected and sorry for herself. One day when Alma corrected her for something, she burst into tears and ran out the door banging it purposefully behind her.

Alma was distressed and couldn't imagine what was wrong with her usually happy, helpful little girl. She went searching for her and found her out by the rosebush, sobbing her heart out as she clung to Girl's neck.

"Nobody loves me, Girl, and nobody needs me," she sobbed into Girl's ear. Girl flicked her ear and gave Neva's wet cheek a comforting lick.

Alma knelt down beside the two. "What's the matter with Mama's girl?" she asked holding out her arms.

Neva looked up, her little face a forlorn study. "Nobody loves me," she sobbed.

"Why, what makes you think that?" Alma asked, her voice soft with love and concern.

"With Lillie here, you don't need me to help you."

"Oh, my darling, I'll always need you." Alma stroked Neva's curls.

"You love Lela more than me!" Fresh sobs shook her small frame. Alma held her close.

I have been so blind, Alma thought. *I've been so busy and so happy to have Lillie around to talk to that I have neglected Neva, I guess. After all we were always together doing things, and she was my only helper. No wonder she feels left out, poor little dear.*

"Neva, you are our firstborn. We had you four years before Lela came. No one could ever take your place, dear. You have your own special place in my heart. I could never do without you. Ralph has his special place in my heart and so does Lela, but there is enough love for everyone."

Neva lifted her face for Mama's kiss and looked at Mama through her tears. The sun shone full on her face and instantly a large gold leaf took form with veins and dew drops. She closed one eye a little and the golden leaf became butterfly wings shimmering in the light. She closed her eye still more and the butterfly wings narrowed into a golden sunset streaked with rays. It became a game. The beautiful golden leaf growing into a butterfly and then diminishing again as she slowly opened and closed her eyes until she forgot the cause of her tears in the joy of her newfound kaleidoscope of gold.

Chapter 14

Butchering

When the busy fall days were over, Lillie returned home, happy with her pretty new dresses. The cabin was quiet and empty without her cheery presence and happy laughter. Alma missed her a lot. She missed her help and the quiet times of girl talk and the fun times. But things soon fell into routine, and Neva and Alma visited together as they worked when Elba was busy outside.

The baby was a happy, healthy little thing. They all enjoyed watching her develop. The first smile, the first goo, the first chuckle were all events to be noted, reported, and enjoyed.

At suppertime one evening Elba announced, "Henry Cudmore is butchering a hog tomorrow. I'm going over to help. Would you and the girls like to come along?"

"Yes, Mama, yes," Neva interrupted. "Please, let's go." She looked pleadingly at Alma.

Elba smiled and said, "It would do you all good."

"It *would* be nice to visit with Harriet and the girls again. Don't suppose I'll have many more chances to get out before winter sets in. Yes, I'd love to go."

"Goody! Goody!" Neva clapped her hands and ran over to Lela's crib. "We're going to go to Lillie's house. 'Bember Lillie?"

"Good! That's settled then," Elba agreed. "We should leave about seven in the morning."

"Wish *we* had a hog to butcher," Alma sighed.

"That's one reason I'm going." Elba leaned back in his chair and hooked his thumbs in his overall braces. "He wants to give us half a hog to pay for those plowshares I sharpened for him last spring."

"Wonderful! We'll have meat enough to do us all winter and more." Alma was delighted.

Next morning the hurry of getting

104

breakfast over, washing the dishes and getting the children dressed kept Alma busy while Elba did the chores and hitched Nettie to the buggy.

The rhythmic clip-clop of Nettie's hooves on the prairie trail and the warmth of the bright fall day made them relaxed and comfortable.

Soon they were driving up the lane to the big white house. The yard was full of children running here and there.

"There's Myrtle and Viola!" Neva jumped up and called, "Hello, Myrtle. Hello, Viola."

The girls came running to meet them. "I like to come to the Cudmores," Neva said happily. "There are so many kids to play with."

Elba tied Nettie to the hitching post. Alma carried the baby inside the house while the girls went to play.

Henry and the boys already had a roaring fire built under the large cast iron kettle. Elba could see the steam rising from the water.

"Hello, Elba. Glad you could make it," Henry greeted him. "You boys get the sawhorses and put some planks on them to make a table."

By this time the little girls and Clarence had come to take in all the excitement of the day.

When the water was boiling and everything was ready Henry sent the girls and Clarence to the house. "You younguns go to the house and tell Ma we need some sharp knives to scrape the hair off the pig."

They dashed away and he called after them, "No fooling around when you're carrying knives."

He turned to Elba. "Now we'll get that pig stabbed while they're away. I don't like the little ones to see the actual killing."

The piercing squeals of the pig as it was caught reached the people in the house and caused involuntary shudders.

By the time the children returned with the knives, the pig had been stabbed and bled, and the men were hoisting it up by a rope and pulley to be lowered into the boiling water.

"Stand back, you kids, so you don't get splashed."

"Does that hurt the pig?" Neva asked concerned.

"No, silly, the pig's dead," Myrtle laughed.

"Are they cooking it?" Neva wanted to know.

"No, they're just scalding it so the

hair will come off." Myrtle was proud of her superior age and knowledge.

Now the men were hoisting the scalded pig out of the water and laying it on the make-shift table. With the knives they began to scrape off the bristles.

The little ones began to laugh and sing:

> Barber, barber, shave a pig
> How many hairs to make a wig?
> Four-and-twenty that's enough,
> Give the barber a pinch of snuff.

They laughed as they wondered what kind of wig twenty-four hairs would make.

Finally, the pig was hung up on the hoist to cool. The men took the washed heart and liver to the house while the boys cleaned up the mess.

Meanwhile the pig was slit down the middle and the innards drawn. Then the women came and stripped and washed the intestines. Some worked alone stripping the intestine through their fingers. Others worked in pairs. One held two steel knitting needles together with the top of the intestine between them. The other pulled the intestine through very carefully lest it be torn.

When they were clean they were put in salt water in preparation for making sausages.

The small intestines made the casing for small farm sausage while the large intestines were reserved for liver sausage.

When the sausage meat was ground and seasoned it was stuffed into the casings and twisted into sausage size rings.

Harriet said, "You men can get washed up on the porch. Lunch is just about ready."

Alma helped the older girls set the table and dish up the food — an enormous platter of fried chicken, another of fried liver and onions, mounds of mashed potatoes, mashed rutabaga, peas and carrots, rich brown gravy, beet pickles and relish.

On the porch the men and boys and little ones were taking turns washing and splashing in the two enamel wash basins, then vying with each other for a dry spot on the long roller towel hanging on the door.

There was the usual pushing and shoving, teasing and poking, scraping of chairs and chatter as the large family was seated around the long table. Then the sudden silence as sixteen heads bowed in reverence and waited for the blessing.

Henry cleared his throat and prayed, "Dear Father, thank you for this good day. Thank you for health and strength and for our kind neighbors who have joined with us. Bless this food we eat. In Jesus' name. Amen."

The happy chatter began again as the nourishing food on that bounteous table was attacked by so many hungry children and adults.

"Please pass the potatoes."

"Just wait your turn."

"Mother, Cecil's taking all the drumsticks."

"Am not!"

"Ugh! Who likes liver?"

"Well pass it on anyway, silly."

"I don't like rutabaga!"

"You have to eat a little bit," Mother's voice interjected. "There's saskatoon berry pie for those who clean up their plates."

When the sumptuous meal was ended, Harriet took Alma into the bedroom for a private talk and prayer. Elba and Henry went back outside to cut the pig in half, and the young people cleared the table and did the dishes. Henry said he would have to butcher again later on so he gave Elba the head and feet.

Neva cried when she had to say

goodbye to the children. Harriet embraced Alma and numerous goodbyes and well-wishes accompanied the little family down the lane.

"That's a lovely Christian family," Elba remarked as he slapped the reins on Nettie's plump flank.

"Harriet is like a second mother to me," Alma said dreamily. "She knows how I feel and always encourages me."

"I like a big family!" Neva declared decidedly. "When I get married I want lots of kids."

"Why's that?" Elba asked.

" 'Cause they have lots more fun. I want a dozen."

"How many are a dozen?" Elba teased.

She threw back her head and smiled at him. "I don't know, Papa, but lots."*

Next day was a busy one. Elba and Alma cut up the meat. Elba made a smoke house and hung up the shoulder and ham to be cured by smoke. Alma pickled the hocks — all except one that she wanted to put with the head for headcheese. The rest of the meat was put in brine in a wooden barrel. The fat was carefully saved, some to be rendered into lard and the rest to be made into lye soap on another day.

*Author's Note: Neva actually had eight children when she grew up.

Chapter 15

Headcheese

"We're going to make headcheese today, Neva," Alma announced one morning at breakfast.

"Headcheese!" Neva snorted. "What's headcheese?"

"It's yummy meat you make from the head of the pig."

"Yuk! I don't like it."

"How do you know? You haven't tried it yet."

"I just know."

Alma took the cleaned pig's head out of the brine where it had been soaking twenty-four hours. The brains, eyes and most of the fat had been removed before it was quartered and placed in the brine.

She placed the quarters in a large pot

and covered them with cold water. Then she put in the cleaned pig's trotter (a pig's foot used as food), an onion, a carrot, a stick of celery, some bay leaves, salt, pepper, one-quarter teaspoon freshly ground nutmeg, and some sage.

When it all began to boil, she skimmed it frequently then let it simmer two to three hours on the back of the stove.

Then she removed it from the stove and allowed it to cool sufficiently for her to strip the bits of meat from the bone.

When Alma was putting it into molds to jell, Neva said, "It smells nice. Maybe I'll try it."

Chapter 16

Making Soap

"I'm going to make soap today and use up the rest of the pig's fat," Alma said one bright morning in early October. "I better get it over with while the weather is still nice."

"Yes, You'll need to make a fire outside, won't you?" Elba agreed. "I'd better stick around today. You'll need help lifting that big kettle."

Alma poured him another cup of coffee. "I'd appreciate that, dear, but I hate to keep you from whatever work you had planned for today."

"Nothing that couldn't wait. I'll work in the shop. That way I'll be handy when you need me."

"Do you think you could whittle me a

big wooden ladle to stir the soap with?" She came over and stood beside him.

"Wouldn't wonder that I could," he said and caught her hand. "How about a little pay in advance?" He pulled her down on his lap and kissed her. "I couldn't exist without you, Alma. You're my life."

She put her arms around him and ran her fingers through his dark, wavy hair. "I love you, too, my big, kind husband. God is so good to us!"

"I'll make the fire for you," Elba said, "as soon as I finish this cup of coffee."

"Thanks. That'll give me time to do the dishes and boil the water." She sang as she worked around the cabin.

Elba loved watching her as she worked, and he loved to hear her sing. Not only because she had a beautiful singing voice but because he needed to know she was happy.

When the fire was burning well, Alma poured boiling water over some wood ashes to make an alkali, which was called potash. Then she put the potash in the large black, iron kettle with the pig's fat and boiled them together.

She stirred it with the large wooden ladle Elba had made for her, trying not to get the mixture on her hands lest it harm the skin.

"Neva, can you bring the frames from the stable for me, please?"

Neva dashed off and soon returned with the frames.

"Now, go and call Papa from the shop. Tell him the soap is ready to pour."

When Elba came, they lifted the heavy kettle together and carried it to the frames.

Elba held out some old pieces of gunny sack.

"Here, use this old gunny sack to hold on to the kettle with so you won't burn your hands."

They poured the hot soap into the wooden frames. As the soap cooled, it hardened and was cut into bars.

"Whew! Glad that's done," Alma said, satisfied. "Enough soap to last a while. It's harsh and doesn't smell like a rose, but it does clean well. So we will be thankful for small mercies."

Chapter 17

Straw Ticks

"It's going to be a hard winter — so the Indians say. Don't know how they can tell, but they're generally right." Elba took his second cup of coffee and sat down in his big wooden rocker. "Glad I got the house banked up before the snow comes."

Whenever Papa sat in the rocker, Neva figured it was an invitation to sit on his knee. She left the table and clambered up.

"Oops! Mind my coffee, Kitten."

Alma looked surprised. "Before snow comes! Surely you aren't expecting snow yet?"

"It's possible," Elba nodded his head.

"For goodness sake! Such a country!

It's only early October."

"It's happened before now," Elba grinned.

"I'd better get those bed ticks down and get them filled with fresh straw."

"Good idea," Elba agreed. "Better be prepared for the worst."

"Let's get the table cleared and the dishes done, Neva. Then we'll bundle Lela up and take her outside with us."

"I'll be working in the shop if you need me." Elba took his cap from the hook near the door. "It'll be good to sleep on a full tick again. My side is sure flat."

"Mine, too," Alma agreed. "It's more like a chaff tick than a straw tick. Where should I empty the ticks, Elba?"

"Dump the straw out on the ash heap. I'll burn it later today."

He went off to his shop to weld a broken wagon rim for a neighbor. Soon Alma heard his merry whistle mingled with the ring of the anvil.

When the breakfast work was finished, Alma and Neva went up the ladder to fetch the ticks.

"I think I'll air the blankets and quilts while I'm at it. You toss them down the ladder for me while I take them off."

It was awkward work getting the

118

ticks down the ladder and out the door. Neva went ahead to get the blankets out of the way so Alma wouldn't trip over them.

They hung the blankets on the line and carried the ticks to the ash heap. With the scissors, Alma picked open the ends where they had been sewn shut. She pulled and tugged to get the old straw out. She turned the ticks inside out and shook them well to loosen all the straw and chaff.

The dust from the straw flew up in her face and made her sneeze. The chaff stuck in her hair and clung to her eyelashes.

It was a dusty, itchy job that she hated, but she knew they would appreciate it when it was all done.

She lifted the round zinc washtub down from the wall and took it inside where she poured water in it placing it on the stove to warm.

"Will we change Lela's tick?" Neva asked.

"We-l-l, she hasn't been sleeping on hers very long. Oh, I guess we might as well. Why not? Then we'll all have a fresh one."

She folded a couple of blankets and put them in a corner for a temporary bed for Lela, who gurgled and cooed her approval.

"I can empty this little tick by myself, Mama."

"Thanks, dear. Be sure you give it a good shake to get all the straw and chaff out."

When the water was warm, Alma carried the tub outside and put it on the box and with the washboard and her homemade soap she scrubbed the ticks until they were clean. She rinsed them and hung them in the sun to dry.

After lunch when the cloth ticks were dry, with Alma carrying Lela and Neva carrying the folded ticks, they made their way to the straw stack.

"Wish we had a baby buggy or a wagon for Lela. She's getting heavy to carry very far."

"Then I could use the wagon too, eh, Mama?"

"Sure, dear," Alma said absentmindedly.

"Mama, how we going to carry the full ticks back?"

"Good question, Neva. I didn't think of that. Maybe we'll have to get Papa to help us."

At the straw stack, Alma laid the baby on the ground and she and Neva

120

began stuffing the ticks with the fresh golden straw.

When the three ticks lay fat and bulging on the ground, Neva said, "Look, Mama, Papa bear and Mama bear and Baby bear."

"Sure enough," Mama laughed. "You stay here and watch Baby. I'll carry your tick home and ask Papa to come and help."

She picked up Neva's single bed tick. It wasn't heavy, but it was big and awkward to carry. She put it up on her shoulder and held it with one hand while she used her cane in the other."

Neva laughed. "You look funny!"

Alma giggled. "At least if I fall I hope I land on the tick."

Soon she and Elba were back, carrying a honey pail of milk and some sugar cookies.

"Time for a picnic," Elba said. They all sat on the ground and enjoyed the goodies while Alma nursed the baby.

Elba playfully picked up a handful of straw and tossed it at Neva. The fight was on! She jumped up and grabbed an armful of straw. Before Elba could move, she had strewn it all over him. They romped and played until they were both hot and itchy.

"I'm all itchy anyway, Papa. Can I slide down the straw stack?"

"Sure. Why not?"

Neva clambered to the top of the stack and slid down time after time.

"Whee! This is fun!"

Alma smiled at Elba. "Not so much fun when she's picking it out of her long stockings and bloomers."

Finally, after brushing and picking as much straw off them as they could, they started home, the double bed tick atop Elba's broad shoulder. Neva struggled along carrying Lela's crib tick, and Alma trailed behind with the baby.

It was a wrestling match getting the bulging ticks through the door, up the ladder, and through the small opening to the loft, but Elba managed.

With needle and thread, Alma sewed up the open ends tightly. Then she put fresh sheets on the beds covering them with the freshly aired blankets.

"We got fat beds!" Neva laughed. "Can I jump on them?"

"No! You can not!" Alma said decidedly. "I know it looks very inviting, but they'll get flat soon enough."

"Yep," Elba agreed. "Come spring they'll be so flat we'll think we're sleeping on the bare boards again."

After supper the washtub was brought in again and water heated for baths to get rid of the rest of the dust and chaff.

"I can't stay on my bed," Neva said as she got into bed. "I roll off."

Alma laughed. "You have to wiggle down and make a little nest for yourself."

Neva wiggled and giggled until she felt comfortable.

When the last of the day's work was done and Alma finally crawled into bed beside Elba, she snuggled down with a deep sigh of contentment.

"What luxury! What pure luxury!" She yawned and stretched her aching body. "Thanks for smoothing my side too, dear. Don't think I'd have enough energy left to do it for myself. I'd probably roll off like Neva."

"You're welcome, darling. You've had a hard day."

"Good night," Alma said dreamily as she drifted off to sleep, tired but content with her day's work. In her nostrils was the delightful freshness of sun-dried, wind-blown sheets.

Chapter 18

Dedication

"This is a big day for our dear Christian friends," Elba said as he urged Nettie along the trail.

"It certainly is!" Alma agreed.

It was a bright mild Sunday in October of 1906, and Elba and family were on their way to the dedication of the Holiness Movement Church about one half mile north of Cannington-Manor.

"These people have sacrificed so much and worked so hard to provide this attractive little church," Alma commented. "I know God is going to bless the service and make the church a lighthouse in the community."

"Just look at all those rigs!" As they drove up to the church, Elba pointed to the numerous buggies and democrats. "Looks like the entire community has turned out. We'll do well to get a seat."

"Do you think it will be all right to leave the pies in the buggy till after service?" Since everyone was invited to the Cudmores for refreshments after the service, Alma had baked pumpkin pies to help out.

"Yes," Elba assured her, "I put a box over them so nothing can get at them."

The church was packed with people of all ages. The "Amen Corner" was filled, and extra chairs had been placed in the aisles and at the back of the church. Elba and Alma found seats near the back.

With shining eyes, Alma took it all in. She loved to come to church. Pastor Clearwater was kneeling at the chair behind the pulpit in silent prayer. To his right sat Brother Cudmore and two other trustees. At the very back of the church sat Brother Cyrenius Fox, his stern countenance and bulky frame intending to discourage any nonsense among the young people.

Besides the feeling of happy excitement and anticipation in the air, there was the unmistakable sense that God was in His house to accept the worship and praise of His people and to bless them.

The congregation sang together the hymn, "O God, Our Help in Ages Past."

Then after a brief prayer, the First Lesson taken from Psalm 84 was read:

How lovely is they dwelling place,
Oh Lord of hosts!
My soul longs, yea faints for the Courts of the Lord:
My heart and flesh sing for joy to the living God.

Even a sparrow finds a home, and the swallow a nest for herself,
Where she may lay her young,
At the altar, O Lord of hosts, My King and My God.
Blessed are those who dwell in thy house, ever singing thy praise!

Blessed are the men whose strength is in thee,
in whose heart are the highways to Zion.
As they go through the Valley of Baca they make it a place of springs;
the early rain also covers it with pools.

They go from strength to strength;

the God of gods will be seen in
Zion.
O Lord God of hosts, hear my
prayer;
give ear, O God of Jacob!
Behold our shield, O God;
look upon the face of thine an-
nointed!

For a day in thy courts is better
than a thousand elsewhere.
I would rather be a doorkeeper
in the house of my God
than dwell in the tents of wicked-
ness.
For the Lord God is a sun and
shield; he bestows favour and
honour.
No good thing does the Lord
withhold from those who walk
uprightly.
O Lord of hosts,
blessed is the man who trusts in
thee! Amen.

How true, thought Alma, *how very
blessed we are. God is so good to us!*

When the trustees were called to
stand in front of the minister, Brother
Cudmore gave an account of the begin-
nings of the church. Henry began in his
shy, sincere way:

128

"Dear friends, as many of you know, I arrived here with my family in 1902. We came from Crystal City where there had been a big revival in the Holiness Movement Church. We opened our home for services.

"Rev. C. W. Doney was appointed in the fall of 1902 by the Holiness Movement to the Saskatchewan Conference. He was our minister for 1902-1903. Then came S. W. Caswell, 1903-1904, T. S. Clark, 1904-1906 and now we have J. S. Clearwater sent to us by this Conference.

"For some time services were held in a store building until our church was built.

"On behalf of the other trustees and the entire congregation, I have pleasure in presenting you this building, to be dedicated as a church for the service and worship of Almighty God."

He handed the key to the pastor, Rev. Clearwater, who requested the congregation to stand as he made the Declaration:

"Dearly beloved, it is meet and right, as we learn from Holy Scriptures, that houses erected for the public worship of God should be specially set apart and dedicated to religious uses. For such a dedication we are now assembled. With gratitude, therefore, to Almighty God, who has signally blessed his servants in their holy enterprise of erecting this Church, we dedicate it to His service, for the reading of the Holy Scriptures, the preaching of the Word of God, the administration of the Holy Sacraments, and for all other exercises of religious worship and service according to the Discipline and usages of the Holiness Movement Church. Amen."

Then the minister led the congregation in a closing prayer:

"Dear God, I repeat the words of Solomon as he dedicated thy house long ago saying: 'O Lord my God, hearken unto the cry and to the prayer, which thy servant prayeth before thee today, that thine eyes may be open toward this house night and day — and hearken thou to the supplication of thy servant, and of thy people Israel, when they shall pray toward this place: and hear thou in heaven thy dwelling place: and when thou hearest, forgive.' Amen"

Chapter 19

Go to the House

Alma watched the early snowfall in October with mixed feelings. How fluffy and soft it was! She remembered a verse she had read:

> I knew it would be white.
> I knew it would be still.
> I knew it would lie molded here
> Upon my window sill.
> And yet I'm not prepared at all
> For winter's first snowfall.

But she also knew that it would mean another long seige cooped up in the cabin with the children. Eventually there would be no more going to church, no more visiting with neighbors. Elba would be gone long dreary days as he hauled wood from the mountains. She sighed as she looked ahead, planning. *I'm going to let Neva outside to play every day possible,* she thought. *It will help to occupy her time. Of course, when it's blizzarding she can't go out.*

"Going to be a hard winter," Elba said one day when he came home from town. "The old Indian who lives north of town said the hull of the corn is very thick this fall. Says he can always tell." He stomped the snow from his overshoes onto the mat. Then he shook the mat out the door letting in a blast of cold and snow.

"Do you think it'll be worse than last winter?" Alma looked out the window as she asked, as though fearing the view had already been cut off.

"Well, the snow has come earlier so it'll seem longer — if it stays." He hung up his bearskin coat and cupped his hands around his ears. "You dread the winter, don't you?" Concern filled his grey eyes as he looked at her.

"It's just that the children and I seem so housebound." She sighed and looked at him seeking understanding. "I hate to think of those long days when you go for wood. I get so lonesome to talk to an adult."

"I know, Alma, I wish it could be

otherwise." He slipped his arms around her. She leaned her head back against his shoulder.

"I mustn't become sorry for myself," she said smiling and turned in his arms to face him. "I am really happy. God has been so good to us. We are all healthy and we have so many blessings. I'm ashamed when I get feeling down, because I know God's grace is sufficient for our every need. I just forget to appropriate it."

"Don't we all?" Elba said, holding her close. "Sometimes I ask God to do something for me; when He does, I even forget to thank Him. I just take it for granted."

"I know what you mean, dear. We surely are stingy with our thanks. God must get fed up with us sometimes." Alma smoothed back his wavy dark hair.

Grey eyes smiled down into brown and just being together was enough.

Snow storm after snow storm came. The wind blowing over the prairie with little to stop it, packed the snow into high hard drifts. Elba didn't have to keep to the trails. He could go anywhere over the vast expanse of white.

"I've never seen the snow so deep," he said one night when he came home from the mountain. "I stood on it today and touched the telegraph wires."

"Elba, is that possible? I can see here in the yard the drifts are high, but I didn't know they would be like that out on the prairie."

"At the back of the house, the drift is up to the eaves. I'm going to put stakes in and string a wire to the barn in case of blizzards. Then I won't lose my way."

"I tried to scratch a hole in the frost on the window today just to see out," Alma said as she busied herself preparing supper, "but the frost was too thick. I was afraid of breaking the window."

"The best way," Elba said, stretching his cold legs out to the fire, "is to take a coin and heat it. It melts the frost and leaves a nice round peephole."

"I'll try that tomorrow. Are there any birds still around?"

"Nothing but the sparrows and magpies. They stay all winter."

"Poor things. Where do they live?"

"The sparrows stay in barns mostly, and magpies stay in the shrubs and bushes."

The days grew shorter. Elba had no sooner finished the morning chores and eaten dinner than it was time to go out again as evening was settling in.

One late afternoon when he was out at the barn, Neva glanced up at the ceiling and shouted, "Mama, our house is burning!"

Alma was sitting in the rocking chair nursing the baby. She looked up and fear welled up in her throat. The stovepipe was red-hot where it went through the ceiling, and the boards all around it were burning. Trying to remain calm and think clearly what she should do, she put the baby in the cradle and grabbed a bucket of water. "Neva, run to the barn and call Papa." The urgency in her voice made Neva hurry.

Alma climbed the ladder and sloshed the water on the burning boards. Down she went for another bucketful and another. Neva came in crying, all covered with snow. "I can't call Papa because I fell down in the snow and I'm all wet and cold."

"Oh, Lord, help me," Alma prayed silently. "I don't dare leave this to call him. Please send him in."

"I'm sorry you fell down, Neva," she said between buckets. "Stay over there and look after Baby."

"I can help, Mama. I can climb the ladder for you," Neva said, running to show Mama.

"All right, maybe that'll be faster." Alma dipped the water out of the barrel and handed the bucket to Neva on the ladder, who climbed the last few rungs and threw the water on the fire. They worked away, mindless of time.

The door opened with a bang and Elba rushed in. He took in the situation at a glance. With long strides he was up the ladder, ripping at the boards and smothering the flames.

"We can thank you that we have a roof over our heads tonight," he said gratefully when the fire was finally out.

"I was so frightened, Elba," Alma said with a little sob. "I sent Neva to call you, but she floundered in the new snow. Poor dear, she came in all cold and wet and so disappointed that she couldn't get Papa. She was a big help to me." She flashed an appreciative smile at Neva.

Elba looked at Neva. Her face was smudged and her dress was wet where she had slopped water on it. "Well, you sure were helping Mama save our home, weren't you?"

"Yep," she said. Then, as reaction set in, "Just lookit this mess!" Elba and Alma had to laugh at the look on Neva's face even though the water and soot covering the floor indeed had made a mess.

As they cleaned up, Alma asked, "Did you hear Neva call, or how did you happen to come in just at the right time?"

"No. I didn't hear her call. God sent me in. I was milking and had this strong feeling that I should go to the house. I went to the barn door and looked out and everything seemed all right, so I went back to finish milking, thinking it was just my imagination. But the impression came stronger than ever, 'Go to the house.' So I did."

"Thank God you did," Alma said fervently. "I was asking God to send you in. That's one more answer to prayer."

Chapter 20

Three Day Blizzard

"Lookit, Mama. My shoe says flip-flop!" Neva flapped her loose sole back and forth.

"Oh, dear!" Alma gasped. "You better put your slippers on before it gets any worse. I hope Papa can fix it. We can't buy new shoes just now."

Neva got her slippers on and came back.

"What can I do, Mama? Neva sighed and went to the window, but she couldn't see out. "Don't like too much snow!"

"I know what you mean. Would you like to play with the button bag?"

"I want to go out."

"It's too cold and windy today, dear."

"No, it isn't, Mama. I want to go outside. Please?"

Alma hesitated. The wind was blowing a gale, yet she knew how Neva loved a run with Girl.

"The wind is so strong; it will blow you away."

Neva laughed. "I'm strong!" she boasted.

"W-e-e-ll, maybe — just for a few minutes."

Neva dashed for her overshoes and wraps. She bundled into her coat and toque and mitts. Alma wrapped a scarf around Neva's neck, pulling it up over her nose and mouth.

"Only a few minutes and don't go far." Alma opened the door. The wind with the strength of an angry giant, snatched the door out of Alma's hand and banged it back against the outer wall.

Neva was pinned against the door jamb gasping for breath. She turned her head from side to side to avoid the wind's persistant force, but it was a suction drawing the breath from her nostrils.

Alma pushed her back into the room.

Neva said in a little voice, "Guess I don't want to go out."

"I guess you don't! Now, I hope I can

get this door closed again."

She went out on the step and grasped the door handle with both hands and tugged with all her might. Eventually the door closed.

"I'd better stir up the fire. That ordeal made the house freezing cold."

A subdued Neva removed her wraps and snuggled down on the braided mat in front of the stove, content to play with the numerous and varied buttons in Alma's collection.

When Elba came in for supper he stomped the snow from his feet and shivered.

"That's a terrible wind out there! It's blowing up a real blizzard." He took off his galoshes and coat and cap and walked over to the stove and put his mitts on top of the warming oven.

"It's good to be indoors on a night like this," he said stretching out his hands to the warmth of the fire. Neva hugged him around the legs. He placed his hands on her shoulders.

"I nearly got blowed away." Neva looked up into his face.

"You what?"

"Oh, she was bound she was going outside," Alma said, disgustedly.

"You didn't let her go out in that

wind, did you?"

"She only got as far as the door and changed her mind, but I had a job to get the door shut."

"You won't be able to go out for a while I'm afraid. I'll get some more wood in here after supper. We might as well settle in for a few days."

"Do you mean you are going to be home for a while?" Alma asked, happiness in her voice.

"Yep, right here or in the shop. No one would travel in this blizzard. They'd be crazy if they did."

"Well, I can almost welcome the blizzard then to have you around the house a bit more. Oh, I forgot to tell you, Neva's shoe has a loose sole."

"I'll fix it after supper." He picked up the baby from her crib.

"How's my little dumpling?" He held her up and tickled her tummy with his nose. She chuckled and grabbed his hair.

"Hey, you're pulling my hair, young lady."

"She does that to me, too," Neva said.

Elba sat in the rocker with both girls on his knee. He began to sing:

My kitty has gone from her basket.
My kitty has climbed up a tree.
Who'll go up among the branches

142

And bring back my kitty to me?

By the time Alma had the supper on the table, Lela was asleep and Neva was dozing. Alma took the baby and laid her in the crib.

"Wake up, Kitten. Time to eat." Elba lifted Neva and placed her in her chair.

Neva yawned and said in a muffled voice, "I'm not asleep."

After supper Elba got his shoemaker's kit. He sat on the wooden horse that had the metal stand. Taking Neva's shoe, he removed the insole and chose a cast iron last the size of the shoe. He placed the shoe on the last and fastened it onto the stand. With his small shoemaker's hammer and shoe tacks, he nailed the loosened sole tightly to the shoe.

When finished, he removed the shoe and ran his finger around the inside to be sure each tack had been clinched smoothly by the metal last. Replacing the insole, he tossed the shoe to Neva.

"There's your shoe, Neva. Good as new."

She put her arms around his neck. "Thanks, Papa. You're the bestest!"

All night long the wind howled around the corners and in its rage rattled anything movable. It scooped up snow and threw it against the window panes.

143

It challenged the sturdy door and swirled snow on top of snow in a frenzy of wild whiteness.

For three days the blizzard raged. The errant sun never made an appearance. The sky was black and heavy and the snowbanks outside the window so high that even during what was supposed to be daylight hours the kerosene lamps were needed.

Once a day Elba braved the raging storm, holding tightly to the safety wire he had strung between house and barn, in order to care for the livestock.

Meanwhile they kept the cabin as snug as possible and enjoyed their forced confinement. Elba was making some rawhide snowshoes and Neva helped, or hindered depending on whose opinion one might have had, but always enjoyed Papa's attention.

Besides the usual work of caring for her family, Alma braided a rug or knitted Christmas presents and just relaxed.

In the afternoon of the third day, the wind spent itself almost as quickly as it had arisen. The sun came out and smiled innocently down on the white sparkling wilderness, just as though it had not played hooky for the past three days.

Chapter 21

Trip to Manor

After the blizzard, the weather turned comparatively mild. Elba resumed his trips to the Moose Mountains to cut cordwood. Neva once more looked forward to her daily frolic with Girl, and Alma was kept busy with Christmas preparations and the usual routine of daily jobs.

Work never ends, she thought to herself. *You'd think in winter with no garden and outside work, things would slow up a bit, but, I declare, I'm always doing something.*

She sighed and went to the door. "If I can't see out the windows, I'll have to open the door and get a look outside these four walls." She wrapped her shawl around her and stood in the open doorway.

Some generous fairy godmother had scattered myriads of diamonds over the surface of the snow. The playful sun touched each one and caused it to sparkle and shimmer. The bushes by the barn were clothed in bridal white. Even the fence posts had donned their ermine caps and the chicken-wire fence wore Queen Anne's lace.

Alma smiled and flung her arms out to embrace the whole exquisite scene.

"What a fairyland!" she said aloud. "Thank you, Lord Jesus, for each breathtaking detail of beauty."

She took a few steps up the steep snow path and turned to look back at the cabin. *It looks like a snow house,* she thought. *From a little distance you'd scarcely know there was a cabin there under all the snow – except for the smoke from the chimney.*

The drifts around the house were so high that they covered the upstairs windows. *No wonder it was so dark in the house!* Alma thought.

At supper that evening after Elba had returned from the mountains, Alma said, "Christmas is coming up pretty quickly. Shouldn't we make a trip to town?"

Elba looked at her, sensing her need to get out of the house. "I was thinking that very thing myself. How about tomorrow if the weather's all right?"

Next day was bright but cold. Elba put the wagon box on the bobsled and scattered some hay on the bottom of the box and covered it with horse blankets. Then he fastened horse blankets over the top of the box.

He heated a large stone in the oven and placed it in the wagon box to keep their feet warm. When Alma and the girls were all packed in and settled, he lit the lantern and placed it near Alma.

"That should keep you warm. Just watch it doesn't fall over and set the hay alight."

"What about you, sitting up there on that wagon seat. Won't you freeze?" Alma asked in concern.

"I'm used to it," he grinned. "Anyway, nothing can penetrate this old bearskin. It's worth its weight in gold." He patted his faithful old coat.

"I'm glad, dear, because the wind goes through my heavy cloth coat as if I had none on."

The bells jingled merrily as the team pulled the bobsled over the pristine snow. It was fun to be riding along snug in their covered sleigh.

"How're you doing back there?" Elba called.

"Fine," Alma replied, "we're cozy." She glanced at Neva who seemed a little off-color.

"Are you alright, Neva?"

Neva nodded her head.

Moments later Neva said, "Mama, I'm s —." She jumped up and ran to the corner of the box and promptly brought up her breakfast.

"Oh, dear!" Alma put the baby down and quickly blew out the lantern. Then she crawled over to Neva and loosened the horse blanket a little to give her some fresh air.

"I'm sorry, dear." She took a clean cloth diaper and wiped Neva's face.

"Guess the fumes got to you, eh?"

"I'm better," Neva said but kept her nose close to the loosened corner of the horse blanket. The fresh air smelled so good.

Arriving in town, Elba helped them out at the general store.

"I'll put the team in Dicken's Livery Stable. I have a few things to get at the blacksmith shop. Then I'll come back here."

To Alma, the general store was a

magical place. She was always amazed at the amount of varied stock that could be packed into such a small space.

She raised her eyes to the crowded shelves that reached right up to the ceiling. She traced the rows of canned goods, groceries, yardage, hats, coats, mitts, shoes, pots and pans, washtubs, buckets, trinkets, knives, guns, ammunition, garden utensils, etc.

They should put up a sign, she thought, *"You Name It, We've Got It."*

She bought sugar, salt, tea, flour, raisins and currants, dried apples, candles, matches, and coal oil.

A couple on-the-side purchases were made when Neva was occupied eyeing the attractive candy jars. Alma could see Neva's mouth almost watering, so she bought some nuts and some peppermint sticks.

Elba arrived and went over to the counter where the shotgun shells were kept. He bought some shells and then had a whispered conversation with the clerk. Alma wondered what it was all about but didn't ask.

"You 'bout ready to go, dear?" Elba carried his purchases in a brown paper bag.

"Neva has to go to the water closet,"

149

Alma said in a whisper.

"Well, let's see. There's one in the station and one in the hotel. Guess the hotel is nearer. I'll help you take the girls over and you can wait there till I bring the team around."

"Elba, please don't forget to go to the post office. Perhaps there'll be a parcel from Mother."

It was warm in the hotel, and as they sat waiting, the heady aroma of roasting beef came to tantalize their nostrils.

"I'm hungry!" Neva declared loudly.

"Sh-h-h. I've got sandwiches in the sleigh. Just wait till Papa comes."

When they were all loaded into the sleigh and had started the trip home, Alma brought out the sandwiches which were cold, but fortunately not frozen. They tasted good!

The wind was in their back, so Elba pulled up the big collar of his overcoat and whistled a tune as he drove the team. Somehow they never seemed to need much urging on the way home.

The lantern wasn't lit on the way home, and of course, the stone was cold, but anticipating what was in the big parcel and letter from Mother and making plans for Christmas kept Alma warm.

Lela was snug and safe in Alma's arms, and Neva was contentment personified. She snuggled down in the hay beside Grandma's exciting big parcel and sucked a delicious peppermint stick.

Chapter 22

Christmas 1906

December 24 arrived with all the wide-eyed excitement and expectancy that accompanies Christmastime, even way out on the prairie.

The Christmas tree was placed in the corner by the ladder and filled the house with its pleasing woodsy smell. They all took part in decorating it, Neva jumping around in her excitement and every few moments dashing over to explain the proceedings to Lela.

Whether she understood Lela's language or not was doubtful, but the chuckles and other happy sounds were sufficient to convince Neva that the baby was enjoying the crackle and buzz of excitement as much as anyone.

When the beautifully wrapped presents were placed under the tree, Neva's eyes shone as brightly as the glittering trinkets on its branches. She clapped her hands and asked, "When do we light the candles, Mama?"

"Just as soon as I finish the dishes. We'll all sit around and enjoy them while Papa reads the Christmas Story. You remember whose birthday it is tomorrow?"

"Yes, it's Jesus' birthday. How old is he, Mama?"

Alma laughed. "That's a good question, dear. It's a long time. He was born many years ago."

"Is he older than Papa?"

"Yes, dear. He's older than Papa."

"In the picture, he's a baby."

"Neva, we celebrate Christmas because that's the time Jesus came to earth as a baby, but he always lived with God in Heaven."

"Was he a baby there?"

Alma lifted a silent prayer for help. How does one explain to a four-year-old such mysteries?

"No, he wasn't a baby until he came to earth."

"Was he big in heaven?"

"I think he was a-a-spirit."

154

"What's a spirit?"

Alma felt she was getting in beyond her depths, so she deftly changed the subject.

"Do you know, we didn't open Grandma's parcel! Why don't you open it and put all the presents under the tree with the others?"

Neva got the scissors and cut the twine and tore off the brown paper wrapping.

There in the box were all kinds of mysterious packages all wrapped in colorful paper. Neva smelled and squeezed and shook each one before she put it down.

One large box caught her fancy. It didn't smell. It didn't rattle. She couldn't imagine what it could be. She looked at the tag. She knew a few printed letters, but this wasn't printing. She carried it to Mama.

"Does this say 'Neva'?"

"Yes. It sure does."

"What do you think it is?" Neva was dancing with excitement.

"I couldn't guess." Alma smiled and gave her a hug.

Elba lit the candles. With the Bible in his hand, he sat down in his rocker. Neva climbed onto his knee. Alma brought the

155

baby and sat in her chair beside Elba.

"The tree looks so pretty," she said, her eyes as bright as Neva's. "I love Christmas!"

Elba squeezed her hand and opened the Bible to St. Luke, Chapter 2 and read the age-old story:

"'And it came to pass in those days, that there went out a decree from Caesar Augustus, that all the world should be taxed.

'And this taxing . . .'"

Alma was lost in the story. She was there on the road with that young couple as they made their weary way to Bethlehem. She saw the concern on Joseph's face and heard his kind voice encouraging Mary. She felt with Mary the anxiety of giving birth to her first baby — in a strange place, far away from mother and those who loved her. She marvelled at the courage of that young girl facing childbirth with only straw for a bed, nothing to relieve her pain and only Joseph's gentle hands to receive her little one into this world.

What a birthing! What a story! What humility! That the great almighty God of the universe, the Eternal One, the Creator of all things should so love us that He was willing to send His Son to earth through this young girl to become a human being — one of us! Surely this was the most wonderful event of all time.

Elba finished the story and prayed.

"Dear Father, we pause in gratitude to thank you for the many blessings you shower upon us. We thank you for daily grace and for your presence with us.

"I thank you for this special time of year and for the gift of your Son. We love Him and want to serve Him.

"I thank you for Alma, for her love and loyalty and because she is so fully dedicated to you and yours.

"I bring you Neva. Thank you for her and all the joy she brings to our home. Bless her. May she ever love and serve you.

"Thank you for giving us Lela. Give us wisdom to care for her and teach her your way.

"In Jesus' name, Amen."

Long before daybreak next morning Neva was awake and stirring. She could dimly make out her long black stocking hanging on the bedpost. It was cold in the room. Papa had not yet built up the fire. She could see her breath.

She hated to get out of her warm nest, but she wanted to see what was in her stocking.

Finally, she threw the covers back long enough to crawl to the foot of the bed, grab her stocking and snuggle back down.

Under the covers, she examined her stocking. She started at the top. She held the top of the stocking and slid the other hand down the stocking. The stocking seemed so long! Down, down went her hand. Nothing! She began to wonder if it would be empty all the way. Down, down — oh, there was something after all. She squeezed it. The paper crackled. It was tantalizing.

She put her hand in and reached down until she touched the paper. She drew it out.

"I wish I could see! It's something soft."

She tore off the paper and examined the gift. There were two. Mitts? No. What's this? She felt something round and soft. A pom-pom! She felt all over one then the other. She put her hand inside one. It was warm. "Slippers!" She said happily and immediately put them on her feet. They fit perfectly and felt so soft and warm.

What else is here, she wondered. She put her hand back in the stocking and felt something round and long. Now what? She pulled it out. She smelled it. No smell. She shook it. No rattle.

She tore the paper off and felt all along the smooth roundness. There was a string half way down. She took the string off and it flapped open. *A book! Oh goody.* She loved books. *Wish I could see! Wonder what kind of book.*

Farther down in the stocking she found a bunch of nuts. She could feel the smooth hazel nuts and the rougher almonds, the round crinkly walnuts and the big Brazil nuts. *M-m-m those will taste good!*

Down to the very toe she felt. There was something wrapped in waxed paper. She hauled it out and smelled it. Maple cream candy!

She opened the paper and popped a piece in her mouth. She lay with her treasures around her happily savoring the delicious sweetness of the maple cream mixed with crunchy walnuts.

Her head came up from under the covers when she heard Alma's voice. "Don't eat all your candy before breakfast, Neva."

Papa stuck his head in the door. "Merry Christmas, Kitten. I'm going to fix the fire, then you can come down when it warms up a bit."

159

"Merry Christmas, Papa. I got lots of stuff!"

"Good!"

Breakfast seemed to take forever to Neva. She wasn't hungry. She couldn't wait for the presents.

"Is it time yet?

"Hurry up, Mama.

"I can't wait."

Finally they were all seated and ready.

Alma expected to see two of Elba's bulky presents wrapped in newspaper, but there was only one. She wondered about that.

Elba picked up the presents, read the names and handed them to Neva to deliver. There were so many presents this year. *Far too many for any one family,* Alma thought.

When all the presents had been distributed, Elba said, "We'll start with the youngest and let her open her presents first while we watch."

Neva grabbed a present and began to open it.

"Wait a minute. I said the youngest. You aren't the youngest anymore, remember?" Elba smiled at her.

"Lela can't open hers," Neva said.

"How about you opening them for

her?" Alma asked.

Neva picked up one and shook it. It gave a loud rattle. "I know what that is." She grinned.

It was a beautiful blue rattle from Grandma.

Lela grabbed it and banged it down on Mama's knee.

"Not so hard, young lady," Alma said. "Do it gently like this."

Neva was unwrapping something soft and bulky. "Wonder what's this? Oh look, Lela. A little doggy!"

Alma had crocheted and stuffed a little dog. It had floppy ears, a black nose and a darling little red tongue.

"He's cute!" Neva said. "Now can I open mine?"

"Yep. You're next."

Neva tore into the big bulky parcel. She pulled the newspaper off to reveal a little red wagon.

"Thank you, Papa!" She threw her arms around him. "I love it! Now we can pull Lela."

"Yes, it will be a big help," Alma agreed.

Neva opened a small soft package and disclosed a pair of red mitts.

"They're pretty, Mama."

Next she found some paints. "Oh,

these are for my coloring book I got in my stocking. Goody!"

The large box from Grandma she opened last. She took the paper off and opened the box, then she gasped, "Oh-h-h." In tongue-tied wonder she examined every detail of a beautiful doll. It had a dainty china head with a smiling face and blue eyes. The body was made of soft kid. It wore a beautiful blue silk dress and slippers. Underneath were frilled lace-trimmed petticoats and underpants. Neva held the doll close. She had never been so happy. She loved her dolly. She loved her grandma. She loved everyone.

"I'll take Lela while you open your presents," Elba told Alma.

Alma found a dainty hanky from Neva, a piece of yard goods from her mother, and a tiny parcel from Elba. She held it in her hands trying to guess what it could be. It felt hard to her touch. She smelled it. It had a faint scent that was somehow familiar. She took the paper off.

"Oh, Elba, how lovely!"

She held up the small blue bottle with the silver trim. "Perfume! I love it. Thank you!" She reached over and kissed his cheek.

"Now you, Papa," Neva said.

There were new braces from Grandma and Grandpa, mitts and a shaving mug from Alma, and a tie rack from Neva.

That night in bed Elba took Alma in his arms.

"Thank you, dear, for a lovely Christmas day. This is our second in Saskatchewan." She knew he was thinking of how different it was for her at her home with all her friends and loved ones around her.

"You miss your home, don't you, Alma?"

She put her hands on either side of his dear face and kissed him.

"I miss my family and loved ones, but Elba dear, this is my home."

They fell asleep in each other's arms.

Chapter 23

Uninvited Guest

The days went by filled with the usual cooking, cleaning, churning butter, baking bread, and washing diapers. Alma didn't try to hang them outside. She dried them on a rack behind the stove. The house was forever full of steamy clothes. So much steam in the air made the frost on the windows thicker than ever.

Neva could usually entertain herself and enjoyed looking after Baby, but sometimes she got restless and Alma had a hard time finding new things to occupy her time.

"What can I do, Mama? Can't I have Girl in the house to play with me?"

"No, dear, Girl is too big and the

house is too small. She'd be jumping around, knocking everything over."

"You said my baby sister would be able to play with me, but she can't even talk or walk."

"Give her time. She has to grow a bit before she can talk or walk, but she will one day. Why don't you get your bubble pipe, and I'll show you how to make soap bubbles."

Neva was up the ladder in a minute and back with her bubble pipe. "Here it is. What do I do?"

Alma made soapsuds in a dish then put the bowl of the pipe in the suds. Lifting the pipe, she blew into the stem, and a beautiful big bubble formed on the bowl. Neva clapped her hands. "Make it bigger, Mama, make it bigger!"

The bubble grew and grew as Alma steadily blew into the pipe. The light from the window caught it and transformed it into a rainbow. "There's fairies in it," Neva said. "I can see their colored dresses." Just then the bubble popped and left a drop of soap suds on the tip of Alma's nose. "That reminds me of a verse I used to know." She recited:

I blew a bubble.

It wasn't any trouble.

A big soap bubble — as big as that.

166

And right in the middle
His wings all a-twiddle
Sat an elf with a fiddle
And a bright pink hat.
He tidied his clothes
And he twiddled his toes
And he scratched on his nose
But he said not a thing.
He just sort of clung
To the bubble and swung.
Then he stuck out his tongue
And the bubble went bing!

"That's just like the fairies in the bubbles! Let me try." Neva took the pipe and dipped it in the suds, but instead of blowing she sucked and got a mouthful of soapy water.

"No, this way." Alma took the pipe when Neva had finished spitting and wiping her mouth and showed her again. "If you put soap on your finger you can take the bubble from the pipe without breaking it."

Neva loved it! She made big ones and little ones. She tossed them up in the air and let them float about the room.

"Wouldn't Girl have fun chasing these, Mama?"

"You can make some in the warm weather so she can."

Neva was blowing a big bubble for

Baby when she heard a footstep outside. "Papa's home. I heard something outside."

Alma stopped her work and listened. "It can't be Papa, or we'd hear the sleigh bells." They both stood silently listening when the door burst open, and a stalwart Indian filled the doorway. His black hair hung in braids on either side of his expressionless face. His buckskin jacket and trousers smelled of stale wood smoke. Moccasins covered his feet, but his hands were bare.

Alma's legs wouldn't support her. She gasped and sank breathlessly into the nearest chair. Instinctively, she wanted to gather her girls in her arms to protect them, but her legs would not obey her commands. Fear welled up in her throat. All the stories she had heard down East about the Indians scalping people came back to torture her. She wanted to speak, but her tongue was as disobedient as her legs. She stared at the intruder with wide, frightened eyes.

Neva, without fear, ran to take him by the hand and pulled him into the warm room, closing the door behind him.

Finally Alma squeaked, "Hello. Can I do something for you?"

The Indian said two words in a

language Alma didn't understand. "Oh, God, please help us now," she instinctively prayed. "What does he want? What is this man going to do?" Her heart was laboring so hard she was afraid he would hear it. *I mustn't let him see I'm afraid,* she thought.

Neva saw the Indian eyeing the fresh bread on the kitchen cabinet. "I think he's hungry, Mama." She ran to the cabinet and got a piece of bread. "You hungry?" She looked up into his face and smiled. She held out the bread. "You want some bread?"

"Bread," the man said in a deep voice. "Bread," he repeated and rubbed his hand over his stomach. A slight smile eased the sternness of his face as he received the bread from Neva. He sat down, back against the wall and ate the bread. Even though he was hungry he didn't wolf it down, but ate delicately, savoring every bite.

When he finished he pointed to the loaves on the cabinet and said, "Bread." Going to the door, he opened it and returned with a basket, the lid of which was beaded in an intricate floral design. He held the basket out to Alma, and again pointed to the bread. "What's he want?" Alma asked, puzzled.

Neva said, "I think he wants to trade the basket for the bread."

"Yes, that's it." Alma went to the trunk and took out a clean flour sack. She put three loaves in it and held it out with a smile. Wordlessly, he accepted the sack and turning to Neva gave her the basket.

"For me?" she asked, delighted. "Thank you. I'll keep it always."

The Indian walked across the room to the cradle. He stood looking down at the baby. Alma held her breath. *What's he going to do now,* she wondered. Lela cooed and gurgled at him. "Papoose," he said, and turned and walked out of the cabin.

"Well, what an experience!" Alma felt drained of all her strength. "I've been wanting a change — a bit of excitement — but I could do without that."

"He's a nice man, Mama. I like him." Neva sat by the fire with her basket on her knee. "It smells smoky, just like him. Wonder what his name is. Wonder how many babies he has. Do you think they'll like our bread, Mama?"

"Well, I should hope so!" Alma looked ruefully at the one remaining loaf of her day's baking. "I'll have to bake again tomorrow."

When Elba came home that night it was a race between Alma and Neva to see who would be the first to tell him about their uninvited guest.

"You can't guess what happened today," Alma began.

Neva interrupted. "An Indian came in. He was hungry." She went to get her basket.

"An Indian?" Elba's face paled. He looked questioningly at Alma.

"Yes. We heard something outside and then he just burst the door open and stood there. I was terrified. I didn't know what he wanted or what he might do. I couldn't speak. I just stood there, then Neva ran up and took him by the hand and pulled him into the room."

Neva came up with her basket. "Look what he gave me. Isn't it pretty? Smell it, Papa."

Elba put the basket to his nose and sniffed.

"Do you like the smell?"

"Yep."

He examined the basket, running his finger over the beaded lid. "Beautiful work. They are wise in so many ways that doesn't come from books. Did he speak English?"

"No, Neva sensed what he wanted.

She gave him a piece of bread. He sat on the floor and ate it quietly. Then he pointed to the loaves I had just baked and said, 'Bread' a couple of times. He rubbed his stomach, and we knew he was hungry and wanted the bread. Then he brought the basket in, and Neva understood that he wanted to trade the basket for some bread."

"Did he say anything else?"

"He said 'Papoose' and walked over and stood looking at Lela in the cradle. Elba, I was petrified. All I could do was pray in my heart. I didn't know what he planned to do. But he just looked at her and then took his bread and left."

Elba was silent for a while. "I suppose the deep snow has made hunting difficult, and the poor folk are hungry. Wonder where he came from. I could spare a bag of wheat for them. I'll ask the Indian who lives near town if he knows him."

"Thank God he was friendly," Alma said with emphasis.

"I understand they mostly are. The English settlement over at Cannington-Manor developed very good rapport with them from the beginning." Elba caught Alma by the hand and pulled her around, grinning roguishly he said, "He'll proba-

172

bly return next spring with a rifle or something to trade for you."

Alma gasped. "Elba Swayze, what on earth are you talking about?"

"Well, the English were so friendly with the Indians that Sha-Wa-Kal-Coosh, son of Chief White Bear, not realizing the difference in the two cultures, arrived one day with his rifle to trade for one of Captain Pierce's daughters. The poor Indian was perplexed when Pierce refused."

"For goodness sake!" was all Alma could seem to say.

"I'll have to take you over to Cannington-Manor one day. They say it's quite a sight. The English came in 1882 and tried to make an English colony on a grand scale for people with 'refined tastes,' but Captain Pierce died and a few years ago it all fizzled out. Fellow by the name of Hewlett lives in the big Humphry's house and farms the land."

"I'd love to go, Elba. Anything about history always interests me."

"I shouldn't have teased you, Alma. I can see you had a frightening time."

"Yes, it was frightening while it lasted, but he meant no harm. I don't know what I would have done without Neva. I think she won his heart, and she seemed to perceive just what he wanted."

Neva felt warm and comfortable at Mama's praise.

"So you were Mama's little interpreter today, eh?"

Neva chuckled. "Oh, Papa, you say such funny things. I'm not a 'terpreter. I'm Neva, don't you know?"

Papa picked her up, hugged her then tossed her up in the air. She laughed and asked for more. "You sure are Neva, and you're special. There's only one like you in the whole wide world, and God gave you to us."